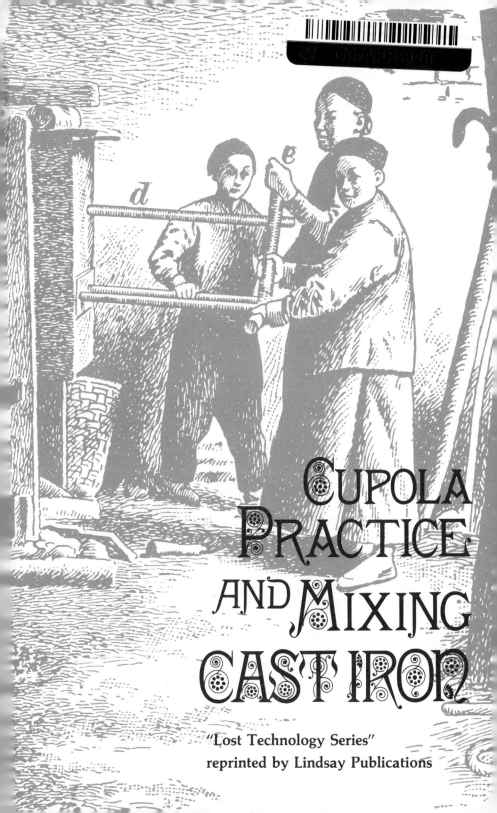

Cupola Practice and Mixing Cast Iron

"Lost Technology Series"
reprinted by Lindsay Publications

Cupola Practice and Mixing Cast Iron

reprinted from a volume published in 1903 by
International Correspondence Schools

Copyright ©1983 by Lindsay Publications, Bradley IL

ISBN 0-917914-12-0

1 2 3 4 5 6 7 8 9 0

INTRODUCTION

Although we may have the impression that the steel industry is a relatively new technology that sprung up in the U.S. in the 1800's, the truth is that the Chinese have been smelting and casting iron for thousands of years.

Today, amateur metal workers want to melt castiron and pour their own castings not only to save money but to gain the satisfaction of having mastered a skill as basic and ancient as iron founding. Mystery surrounds the melting of iron. The high temperatures make it appear difficult. But if it is so difficult, how could it have been mastered centuries ago with the most primitive of tools? What are the secrets?

In this reprint you'll learn the secrets of the cupola furnace which is probably the simplest reliable furnace for melting iron, a furnace that is rarely seen anymore. As you'll see, cupolas constructed from an old wooden flour barrels lined with fire brick have successfully melted iron. Learn the secrets of basic construction, operation and maintenance.

In the second part, learn how a foundryman at the turn of the century would have chosen scrap iron for melting in his cupola so that he could obtain the metal characteristics he needed. Metallurgy has changed much since then, so some of the recommendations and pointers may be obsolete or difficult to implement. Other general principles, no doubt, still apply.

What you get in this unusual reprint is raw information from experts who were writing at a time when the cupola was state-of-the-art. You get a chance to "pick their brains" and go back in time to obtain rare information that will help you enjoy your metalworking hobby.

WARNING

Remember that the materials and methods described here are from another era. Workers were less safety conscious then, and some methods may be downright dangerous. Be careful! Use good solid judgement in your work. Lindsay Publications has not tested these methods and materials and does not endorse them. Our job is merely to pass along to you information from another era. Safety is your responsibility.

Write for a catalog of other unusual books available from:

Lindsay Publications
PO Box 12
Bradley IL 60915-0012

CUPOLA PRACTICE.

APPLIANCES FOR MELTING IRON.

CUPOLAS.

INTRODUCTION.

1. Kinds of Furnaces for Melting Iron.—There are two distinct forms of furnaces used for melting iron. One, called a *cupola furnace*, is shown in Figs. 1, 2, 3, and 4; in this furnace the iron and fuel are charged together. The other form of furnace, called a *reverberatory*, or *air*, *furnace*, is shown in Fig. 13 (*a*) and (*b*), and in it the iron and fuel are charged in separate chambers. The **cupola furnace,** or **cupola,** is the more convenient and economical one for melting, and is the furnace generally used. While this statement is true in general, there are conditions under which the cupola is less effective than the air furnace. These conditions exist where the strongest grades of cast iron are desired, or where large bodies of scrap iron, such as anvil blocks, pieces of large rolls, or cannon, are to be melted, or where it may be desirable to obtain large amounts of metal at one tapping.

2. Operating a Cupola.—There is much more experience, skill, and care required in melting iron in an air furnace than in a cupola; and failures to melt iron successfully, which are more frequent in air furnaces than in

§ 46

cupolas, cause considerable extra expense. With cupolas
the risks to be run are not so great.   If the heat fails to be
successful in a cupola, the damage is as a rule very small
compared with what it may be in the air furnace.   For this
reason there is less risk to operate a cupola than an air furnace, and, in fact, with a study of the principles involved in
the management of cupolas, any fairly intelligent person
should after a little experience become proficient in operating them.

CONSTRUCTION OF CUPOLAS.

3. Form and Dimensions of Cupolas.—The style
of cupola shown in perspective in Fig. 1 is constructed of
sheet iron ranging from $\frac{3}{16}$ to $\frac{3}{8}$ inch in thickness.   It has a
wind belt a, with openings b in the outer casing opposite
the tuyeres c.   By uncovering the holes b, a bar may be
introduced to clean the tuyeres c, or the condition of the
inside of the cupola may be observed through small mica-
covered openings in the covers of the holes.   A drop bottom
d, d is used for the purpose of emptying the cupola at the
end of a heat.   Cupolas are usually made from 22 to
100 inches inside diameter, and generally have stacks of the
same diameter as the portion below the charging door e,
as shown in Fig. 1.   The top of the stack has a hood f that
prevents the rain and snow from entering the cupola, and
also to some extent prevents the sparks from passing out.
Though the majority of cupolas are made from 22 to 100 inches
inside diameter, there are a good many that are less than
22 inches; and in the United States there are a few cupolas
that are over 100 inches in diameter.   Small cupolas are
used to melt iron for making tests; they are also used in
foundries, such as those making iron bedsteads, where melted
iron is required throughout the day, but in such small quan-
ties that cupolas as large as 22 inches in diameter will melt
it too fast for the work.

The larger a cupola is in diameter, the higher it can be
made.   The height of a cupola is generally considered to be
the distance from the bottom plate g, Fig. 1, to the sill of

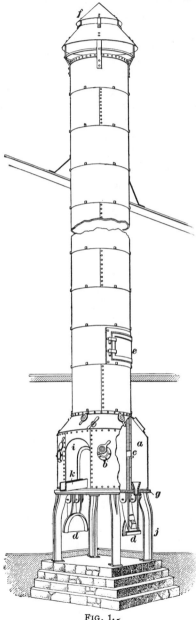

FIG. 1.

the charging door e, and, ordinarily, the height to the charging door should be $3\frac{1}{2}$ times the inside diameter for cupolas between 30 inches and 40 inches, and from this up to 60 inches, 3 times the diameter, and so on according to size. The most important part of a cupola is that part below the level of the charging door; that above it is merely for draft and to convey the sparks, gases, and smoke above the roof, so that they may be discharged clear of the building.

The modern tendency is to increase the distance between the tuyeres c and the charging door e; the advocates of this method claim greater fuel economy and more uniform melting than are secured in cupolas having the charging door located lower.

It is desirable that the interior of cupolas be provided with angle irons b, as shown in Fig. 2. These support the firebricks that are used to line the cupola, in sections, any one of which may be torn out for repairs without disturbing or injuring the other sections.

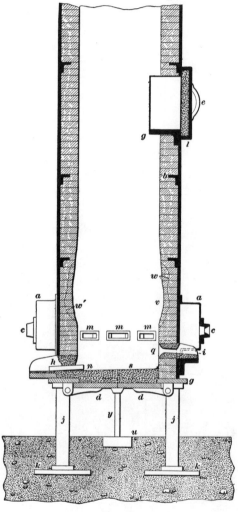

Fig. 2.

4. Wind Belt of a Cupola.—The **wind belt** of a cupola, shown at a, Figs. 1 and 2, should have its cross-section

at least equal in area to that of the tuyeres which are supplied with air through it.   The wind belt has openings *b*,
shown in Fig. 1, and *c*, shown in Fig. 2, opposite the tuyeres *c*,
shown in Fig. 1.   These permit the progress of the melting
to be watched, and also the tuyeres to be opened by means
of a bar passed through the openings, so that the blast may
reach the incandescent fuel, should the metal become chilled
or the tuyeres closed up.   It is well, also, to have the wind
belt arranged so that a portion of the side or bottom can be
removed to take away any slag or iron that runs through
the tuyeres into it.   The iron for forming the wind belt may
range from $\frac{1}{8}$ to $\frac{3}{16}$ inch in thickness.   The wind belt may
be cut off, as shown in Fig. 2, or made narrow at the front
of the cupola, or it may be built with an opening around the
spout *h*, as shown at *i*, Fig. 1.   This form of construction
is also necessary at the rear of the cupola, where slag holes
are located.   The foundation plate *g*, Figs. 1 and 2, is generally made of cast iron, and ranges in thickness from 1 to
3 inches, according to the size and weight of the cupola.
The supporting columns *j*, Figs. 1 and 2, under the cupola
should extend below the level of the floor from 1 to 2 feet
and rest on a solid stone or brick foundation, as shown at
Fig. 1, or on large and thick iron plates, as shown at *k*, *k*,
Fig. 2.

5. ˙ **Construction of the Charging Door.** — The
charging door of a cupola is sometimes made with a
flange *l* projecting inwards about 2 inches around the edge,
so that the interior of the door may be lined with firebrick or
fireclay, as shown in Fig. 2.   Charging doors are also made
without any lining for fire protection, and one of the most
serviceable charging doors is made of heavy iron-wire screen.
Charging doors are hinged, or are arranged to slide vertically by means of chains and counterweights; very large
charging doors are sometimes mounted on wheels that run
on a track on the charging floor.

6. **Tuyeres.**—The **tuyeres** are the openings, shown
at *c*, Fig. 1, and *m*, Fig. 2, that convey the blast from the

wind belt a to the interior of the cupola and are arranged in one or more rows around it. The rows of tuyeres may be horizontal, or the tuyeres may extend in one spiral row, as shown at a', c', etc., Fig. 3. Coke and coal are the two kinds of fuel generally used for melting iron in cupolas; a cupola designed to use coke for fuel should have a larger tuyere area than one designed to use coal. The larger area of tuyeres for coke melting is necessary because of its greater tendency to chill and also because it burns quicker than coal, and thus requires more air. When the fuel chills at the tuyeres, the slag and metal falling on it chill also, and enter the openings between the pieces of fuel and rapidly close the tuyeres and prevent the air entering the cupola.

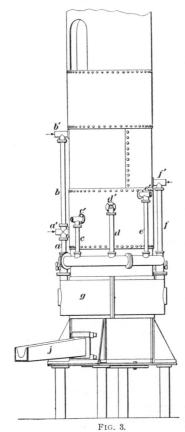

FIG. 3.

Tuyeres have been constructed of nearly every conceivable form, but the rectangular and circular forms are the only ones now generally used. It is a good plan to have the tuyeres widen horizontally from the shell of the cupola to the face of the lining. The tuyeres are sometimes set so as to slope downwards into the cupola to prevent any melted iron from dropping into them. The combined area of all the tuyeres at their smallest section should not be larger than 25 per cent., nor smaller than 15 per cent., of the area of the cupola. This rule includes the upper as well as the lower tuyeres. The longer the cupola is intended to be in blast at each heat, the larger tuyere area it should possess.

7. Height of Tuyeres.—The height of the tuyeres above the bottom of the cupola is dependent on two conditions; viz., the length of time a cupola is intended to be in blast at each heat, and the greatest amount of iron that may be required at any tapping. The majority of cupolas run from 1 to 3 hours per heat, and the iron is let out either as fast as it melts by having an open tap hole, or by tapping it at short intervals. In cupolas working under the conditions just mentioned, and using coke for fuel, the bottom of the tuyeres can be placed from 10 to 20 inches above the foundation plate, and from 8 to 10 inches when coal is used. Where cupolas are run over 3 hours, or larger bodies of metal are desired at one tapping than can be held in low-tuyere cupolas, then the tuyeres must be placed higher.

The reason that high tuyeres assist in running long heats is that they admit of a greater space below the level of the tuyeres to hold the slag and other refuse matter that comes from the fuel and iron. As an example, cupolas for melting iron at steel works that run day and night for a whole week must have high tuyeres. ⸍ Sometimes upper tuyeres are used in connection with lower ones, to aid in obtaining long heats.

8. Height and Position of Slag Holes.—In cupolas made to run long heats, the bottom of the lower tuyeres is generally from 30 inches to 60 inches above the foundation plates. This height admits of placing the slag holes, which are for the purpose of drawing off the slag from the melted portion of the charge, 10 inches to 15 inches below the level of the bottom of the lower tuyeres. This distance of the slag holes below the tuyeres prevents the slag from rising up to a point where the influence of a cold blast can have any effect in chilling it and thus retard its free discharge from the cupola during the process of melting. When the top of the slag holes is placed within 2 or 3 inches of the bottom of the tuyeres, the slag must rise up so close to the cold blast before it can escape, that it will be chilled or thickened to such a degree that it cannot flow freely from the slag hole. This thickening of the slag at the level of the slag hole, caused by the cold blast chilling it and so preventing its free escape from the cupola, may cause it to rise rapidly to the level of the tuyeres, where it may then be so thoroughly chilled as to completely close the openings between the pieces of fuel about the tuyeres and so allow little or no blast to enter the cupola.

9. Long Heats in a Cupola.—The success of steel works and foundries in running **long heats** depends on the removal of the slag or refuse from the body of incandescent fuel before it reaches a level where the cold blast, as it enters the cupola, has any chilling effect on it. The objections to high tuyeres are that the cupola requires more fuel than one using low tuyeres, since the fuel below the level of the bottom tuyeres is of little value in increasing the heat above the bottom tuyeres, where the melting takes place, and also a cupola having very high tuyeres cannot produce as hot or fluid iron as one having lower tuyeres. Hence, unless high tuyeres are a necessity to give a good position to the slag holes, greater economy in the use of fuel when running small heats and hotter iron can be obtained by placing them as low as possible. In locating slag holes, they should be placed on the side of the cupola opposite to the spout and tap hole and between the tuyeres, so that, should the slag come up sufficiently near the level of the tuyeres to be affected by the blast, it cannot influence its free discharge, as will happen if the slag hole is placed under a tuyere. A slag hole is formed in a cupola by placing a 2-inch round gate stick in a 4-inch to 5-inch square or round hole made in the brick lining of the cupola, and packing damp clay around the stick to form a hole of the form shown at q, Fig. 2. A spout i is necessary to carry off the slag to a sand basin in the foundry floor, or into a car or ladle. One method to remove the slag is to collect it from the spout in a clay-lined iron box on a truck, a large eyebolt being set in the molten slag. After the slag hardens, it is lifted from the box by means of a crane and deposited on a car and hauled to the dump.

10. Upper Tuyeres in Cupolas. — Upper tuyeres may be round or square, and are usually placed from 10 to 16 inches above the lower tuyeres; the lower the blast pressure, the nearer to the lower tuyeres should the upper ones be placed. The combined area of the upper tuyeres should be from two-tenths to three-tenths as much as that of the lower tuyeres.

11. Multiple Rows of Tuyeres. — Some cupolas have two or three rows of upper tuyeres, and others have them arranged in the spiral form shown in Fig. 3. Windpipes a, b, c, d, e, f, etc., Fig. 3, convey the air to the upper tuyeres a', b', c', etc. The lower tuyeres receive the air directly from the wind belt g. It is best to have some arrangement of valves whereby the blast entering the upper tuyeres can be regulated or shut off entirely, as may be convenient; furthermore, it saves the lining of the cupola if the blast is shut off entirely from the upper tuyeres toward the close of a heat.

12. Advantages and Disadvantages of Upper Tuyeres. — While it is admitted that properly arranged upper tuyeres save fuel and also increase the speed of melting, as well as assist in extending the length of heats, a drawback to their use is found in the fact that they cause the lining of the cupola to burn out faster than when they are not used. Hence, some founders have closed the upper tuyeres of their cupolas in the belief that the tuyeres caused a greater loss of money for daubing clay and firebricks than they saved for fuel. Where daubing clays are expensive, and the linings are cut out badly by the use of upper tuyeres, this may be a good practice to follow. The success in cupola practice does not really depend on the shape of the tuyeres, but on furnishing the cupola with the proper volume of air evenly distributed. This has been done successfully in large cupolas, not by the spiral arrangement of the tuyeres, but by making the lower tuyere continuous around the entire circumference of the cupola.

13. Center Tuyeres.—In Fig. 4 is shown a tuyere in the center of the cupola, which is a form sometimes used

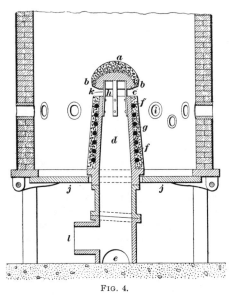

in cupolas above 66 inches inside diameter. A center-blast tuyere requires a cap *a*, as shown in Fig. 4, to prevent the iron and fuel from entering it. It is difficult, in using a center tuyere having a cap *a*, to prevent the points *b, b* from being broken by the friction of the charge in descending during the melting operation. To overcome this difficulty, it is necessary to have the iron cap *c* studded

FIG. 4.

with fingers or prickers on its upper surface, which project outwards about ¾ inch, and, when daubing the cap with fireclay, to fill the spaces between the prickers full and even, as shown in Fig. 4. The clay, after having been daubed on, should be well dried either by having the cap and body *d* of the tuyere placed in an oven, or dried in the position shown in Fig. 4, by building a small fire at the bottom opening *c*. After the tuyere has been dried before being subjected to the action of great heat, it will require but little clay thereafter to patch and keep it in working order. The body *d* of a center tuyere, shown in section in Fig. 4, is made of cast iron with several rings *f* shrunk on the outside, which hold a coating of from 3 to 4 inches of fireclay *g* daubed on the tuyere to protect it from the heat when melting.

The opening at h for admitting the blast to the cupola should be from $2\frac{1}{2}$ to $3\frac{1}{2}$ inches high, and should be located about 4 inches above the tuyeres i in the side of the cupola. The opening of the center tuyere, being higher than the tuyeres i in the shell of the cupola, serves to promote perfect combustion to some extent like the upper tuyeres in the form of cupola shown in Fig. 3. The center tuyere shown in Fig. 4 is a permanent structure, the drop doors j,j being hinged so as to drop away from the tuyere. The cap a is supported by iron bars k that are fastened to the iron body d. The air enters the center of the tuyere through a pipe l at the bottom.

LINING CUPOLAS.

14. Laying the Bricks in a Cupola Lining.—In laying the bricks to line a cupola, the closer the joints are made, the better, since the bricks commence to cut or burn at the joints. If the joints are open, the flame and hot gases, under the influence of the blast, get between the bricks, causing a much greater destruction of the lining than if the joints were narrow and close. The bricks should be laid in the best quality of fireclay, which should be thoroughly mixed with water and made thin enough to pour readily from a dipper. Each layer of bricks should be bedded on the clay grouting quickly, before it has time to stiffen. As each brick is laid, it is a good plan to strike it lightly with a hammer, as this brings it to a solid bearing. Instead of using a dipper to spread the thin clay, the bottom and one end of each brick may be dipped into the clay grouting before being laid. Another method is to pour the clay by means of a dipper on the course of bricks that has been laid and then dip one end of each brick for the next course in the grouting and hammer it to a tight joint against the course under it and the end of the brick just preceding it in the same course.

In order to cheapen the grouting, sometimes about 1 part of silica, fire, or other clean sharp sand is mixed with 3 parts of clay, but this ought not to be done unless the clay is very rich. A clearance of from $\frac{1}{2}$ to $\frac{3}{4}$ inch should be left between the bricks and the shell of the cupola. This space is then filled with grouting made of about equal parts of clay and sand, since the grouting for this purpose does not have to be as strong as that used between the joints of the bricks.

15. Single and Double Lining.—Cupolas are lined either with single or double courses of bricks. It is often better to line with double courses; then, when the inner one burns out, it can be replaced without disturbing the course next to the shell. Also, by having a double lining, the risk of burning through during the process of melting is avoided.

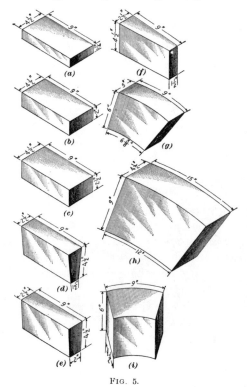

FIG. 5.

The outer course of bricks may be of a much cheaper or poorer quality than the inner one.

16. Forms of Bricks for Linings.—Fig. 5 shows the common forms of firebricks that are used for lining cupolas. The two bricks shown in Fig. 5 (*a*) and (*b*) are called *split bricks*, which are thinner than the regular 9-inch firebrick shown in Fig. 5 (*c*). The bricks illustrated in Fig. 5 (*d*) and (*e*), which taper from edge to edge, are called *side-arch bricks*, while the one shown in Fig. 5 (*f*), which tapers from end to end, is called a *wedge brick*. In Fig. 5 (*g*) and (*h*) are shown two sizes of *circle bricks*, and in (*i*) is shown a *block brick*.

When circle bricks or block bricks are used, they should have a radius exactly equal to that of the cupola. In general, the larger sizes of bricks give the best service for the reason that there are fewer joints to be attacked by the flame and heat during the process of melting.

The bricks for the lower portion of cupolas where the iron is melted should be of the best fireproof composition; these are generally softer in texture than the poorer quality of brick. Hard, close, dense bricks do not stand long usage in the melting portions of the cupola. The hard bricks are placed above the melting zone, as they will stand the abrasive action of the iron and fuel better than soft bricks. For the stack, cheap grades of firebrick are used; common red bricks are sometimes used for stacks and also for the outer course in laying the lining in the body.

17. Other Materials for Linings.—A number of attempts have been made to secure a lining that will resist heat better than bricks made of fireclay, and for this purpose silica, ganister, magnesia, asbestos, and carbon bricks are sometimes used. It is claimed that carbon bricks made of fine coke mixed with fireclay having tar for a binder have proved an excellent material to withstand high temperatures. Fireclay bricks are composed chiefly of silica and alumina. The more silica a fireclay contains, the better it will resist a high temperature. Some manufacturers claim that they make firebrick with the silica as high as 90 per cent. and having alumina for a binder. When bricks contain more than 70 per cent. of silica, they are generally very friable and disintegrate readily, and while they will work well in the melting portion of the cupola, they will not last long if placed near the charging door, where they have to withstand the abrasive action of the fuel and iron. Silica is an oxide of silicon, of which white sea sand is an example, and requires the addition of some plastic material as a binder when used for bricks.   Nearly all clays are composed chiefly of silicate of alumina, which, while having a lower melting point than silica, works well when mixed with it.   There are other substances besides silicate of alumina in the clay, among which are iron oxides, magnesia, soda, and potash, most of which, to some degree, reduce the durability of firebricks.   The silica in firebricks should be of pure quartz or anhydrous silica.   The purchaser should have a chemical analysis of the bricks in addition to a knowledge of their physical qualities to assist him in forming an opinion of their durability.

18.   Causes of Destruction of Linings.—When firebricks are used for the lining of a cupola, they are gradually destroyed by the action of the heat and flame from the fuel and by the sodium chloride and other alkaline substances in the coke.   The bricks are also worn away by the abrasive action of the iron, fuel, and fluxes as they descend from the charging door.   A third factor in the destruction of a cupola lining is the pressure of the blast used.   A strong blast may prove very destructive to the lining when there is little iron in the cupola or when the charge is not sufficiently close to prevent the blast from passing up between the charge and the lining.

Relining a cupola is expensive work, and too much care cannot be exercised in the purchase and use of firebricks. The life of the firebricks is also greatly increased by proper picking out and daubing up the cupola, operations that are described later on in the text.

19.   Drying the Lining.—After a cupola has been lined it should be dried, so as to drive the moisture out of the bricks and grouting as completely as possible before melting iron.   If this is not done, the lining will be found burned out much more after the first heat than it otherwise would have been.   Drying the lining prevents the great difference in the expansion of the inner and outer parts of the bricks, which would otherwise occur when the surface next to the fuel is suddenly highly heated.   The drying process also drives out the greater part of the moisture and prevents the rapid creation of steam, which, combined with unequal expansion, causes the outer surface of the bricks to spall or flake off when suddenly heated. This effect is greatest at the points of highest temperature and in hard dense bricks. Soft bricks allow the steam to be liberated easier and are also more yielding to differences in external and internal expansion.

20. Starting the Fire for Drying a Cupola Lining. In starting a fire in a cupola to dry out a new lining, the drop doors *d*, *d*, shown in Fig. 2, are closed and covered with sand to a depth of from 2 to 3 inches, so as to prevent the heat from warping the doors. This having been done, shavings or other light combustibles are placed on the bottom sand *s*, and over this fine kindling wood is set in an open manner, so as to permit it being kindled easily, and on the top of this fine kindling, heavier combustibles are placed so as to form an open foundation for coke or coal, the charge of the latter fuels being from 12 to 18 inches in depth. The shavings are ignited by means of the red-hot end of an iron rod pushed through the breast of the cupola. After the fire is well under way and the coke burning, more fuel should be added to form a solid bed of ignited fuel about 2 feet deep. Finally, all the draft passages should be closed and the fire left to burn out before dropping the bottom to get the cupola ready for a heat.

21. Treatment of the Lining Before the First Heat.—After the drying fire has burned out, and the bottom *d*, Fig. 2, is dropped and the cupola cooled off a little, it is a good plan to go over all the surface of the lining with a thin grouting of fireclay, using a handful of salt in the pail of water used to wet the clay. The grouting can be put on with a brush and should be rubbed well into all the joints of the lining. This treatment will help to put a glaze on the face of the lining, which is very beneficial in resisting the cutting out or burning effect of the first heat, which is always harder on the lining than any that will follow. It is also advisable in the case of a new lining to get the second fire started as soon as practicable after the first, and also to let it burn as long as possible before starting the blast. The shorter the first heat can be made the better, and care should be taken to keep the blast as mild as practicable. By following these directions, the least amount of a new lining will be burned out during the first heat.

CLEANING THE CUPOLA.

22. First Operation in Cleaning a Cupola.—After a heat has been run off in a cupola, the dropping or dump

FIG. 6.

has to be removed. This is either pulled out from under the cupola, at the time the bottom is dropped, or shoveled out by hand 6 to 12 hours afterwards, when it has cooled. The refuse sticking to the lining is next chipped or picked off by using two small hand picks of the form shown in Fig. 6; the first one should weigh about 2½ pounds and the second one about 1¼ pounds. The heavier pick is to be used in the rough work, and the small pick for finishing up.

23. Necessary Precautions in Cleaning a Cupola. In picking out the refuse, care should be taken not to remove the glaze or cinder coating of the lining. The glaze that a heat or two will create on the surface of the lining will generally protect it as well, if not better, than the daubing. In picking out a cupola, the surface of the melting zone should be kept in as good a form as possible. Any humps that may form above the tuyeres to distort the melting zone from the form shown at *v*, Fig. 2, are very injurious to the lining and to the speed in melting. All such humps, whether hard or soft in structure, should be carefully removed by using the heavy pick for the rough work and the light one to even up the surface.

24. Bunged Cupolas.—Sometimes a cupola, when operated beyond its capacity, or if not properly charged, or owing to some accident, **bungs up** so badly that one cannot enter it to repair the lining. In such a case a hole is made through the center of the bunged portion by means of heavy pointed bars introduced through the charging door. After a hole has been made with the bar, a heavy sledge may be used to knock down the refuse hanging to the lining, and the work may then be finished with the picks, which should be well tempered and sharpened so as to remove the refuse easily and without jarring the glazing of the lining.

MELTING ZONE OF A CUPOLA.

25. The conditions necessary to bring iron to the fusing point are definite and fix a certain place in the cupola as the **melting zone**, or point at which the charge melts. This zone starts from 5 to 8 inches above the top of the tuyeres and extends upwards 10 to 14 inches, according to the character of the fuel, the iron used, the pressure of the blast, and the internal diameter of the cupola, which is enlarged in the melting zone. To obtain the best results in melting, it is very essential to keep the melting zone in proper form. The area of the melting zone should enlarge gradually from the lower edge until it reaches the maximum size, and then contract gradually towards the upper edge of the zone, as shown at v, Fig. 2. It is a common occurrence for the melting zone to burn out and have the forms shown by the dotted lines at w and w', Fig. 2. Either of these forms will cause bad melting, on account of the depressions being too great. The upper part w, being so much larger in diameter than the balance of the melting zone, does not give the descending stock a chance to expand outwardly and properly fill the abrupt depression. The abrupt depression, shown at the lower part of the dotted line at w', often causes the iron to form a bridge over the tuyeres in such a manner that it prevents the charge from descending. The cavity formed at w permits the blast to escape up the sides of the cupola, instead of being spread or forced outwards through the descending charges of fuel and iron, thus causing an escape of heat that should have been utilized in melting the iron. Not only does the escape of the blast in this manner at w retard the speed of melting, but it also causes the lining of the. melting zone and portions above it to be burned out much more than will occur if the blast is forced through the body of the charge. Also, the more the blast cuts out the lining, the more dirt there is formed in the charge, and this decreases the speed of melting and causes the cupola to become bunged up. Hence, the blast escaping between the charge and the lining of the cupola prevents economy in the use of fuel, and also prevents the cupola from producing hot metal, doing fast melting, and making clean and successful heats.

It is very important, therefore, that the surface of the melting zone form a gradual slope in both directions from the longest diameter at the center, as shown at v, Fig. 2, towards the upper and lower edges of the zone, which are of the same diameter as the cupola lining. Not only should the slope be gradual in both directions, but care should be taken to prevent the melting zone becoming enlarged to any great degree; for if this occurs, although the slope may be gradual, the extension in area may be so great that the stock cannot adjust itself to the enlargement sufficiently to prevent too much of the blast escaping between the sides of the lining and the charge. Melters, as a rule, do not give sufficient attention to keeping the melting zone in correct form, forgetting that it is really one of the most important factors in controlling the results in melting.

26. Repairing the Melting Zone.—In repairing the melting zone, care should be taken not to make its diameter less than that of the cupola lining, for this is smaller than it should be and is a condition that may cause the lining to cut out very badly in a single heat. In all cases where the lining has been repaired, it is well to start the fire as long before putting on the blast as possible, so as to give the repaired part a good chance to dry before the high temperature for melting the iron is reached. The lining above and below the melting zone, if of good bricks and well laid, should last from 9 to 12 months, or more, with a heat every day; and if the melting zone is kept repaired and in proper form, it will remain in good condition for melting iron as long as the rest of the lining.

<hr/>

DAUBING A CUPOLA.

27. General Method of Daubing a Cupola.—The cupola having been picked out to the proper form, the next operation is to fill up all the holes and daub the surface of the melting zone with clay, so as to prevent the lining from being excessively burned out during the process of melting. The material used for daubing should be as refractory as possible. The best materials for this purpose consist of a good grade of fireclay and sharp sand mixed together; the proportions depend on the character of the clay and the sharpness of the sand. The aim should be to obtain a daubing that will crack as little as possible in drying and when subjected to the high temperature when melting the iron. Nearly all kinds of clay will shrink and crack if used alone, but a mixture of sand and clay can be used for daubing that will crack very slightly when drying or when exposed to high temperatures.

28. Mixing the Materials for Daubing.—When the daubing for a cupola is made of clay and sand, they should be mixed together from 10 to 15 hours before using. Both the clay and sand should be dry, and the mixing should be done before the water is added. The mixing of sand with wet clay will not make a good homogeneous daubing, and the clay will crack in spots and some of the sand will be released when the mixture becomes heated, and either of these defects will reduce the value of the daubing.

Some clays are much more plastic than others, so that the amount of sand required to be mixed with them has to be found by trial. Some clays may be so plastic as to require one-half sand, while others need only one-quarter; and some clays are so friable, possessing little or no plastic qualities, that they will not admit of any sand being mixed with them. A daubing should be so plastic that it will stick together well while being used. The clay should be as stiff as it can be handled, since the stiffer it is, the less moisture or steam there will be to expel during the process of drying. At the very best, the conditions are unfavorable to the escape of

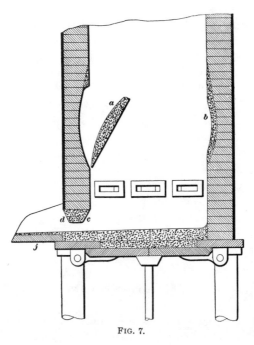

FIG. 7.

moisture or steam from the daubing, and where there is much formed, it will, in escaping, have a tendency to press the daubing outwards from the lining. The surface of the daubing exposed to the fire or blast forms a hard glazed crust through which the steam cannot pass; the steam will then tend to separate the daubing from the lining, often causing it to fall away at the commencement of the heat, as shown at *a*, Fig. 7.

29. Other Daubing Mixtures.—Instead of using fireclay mixed with sharp sand for daubing, some founders use common blue or yellow clay; some of these clays work fairly well when mixed with sharp sand. New molding sand, or loam, wetted with clay wash, or a loam without mixture with any other material, is sometimes used. Where good loam sand can be obtained, it may serve in the place of better material; but molding sand by itself is worse than nothing, as it only dries to a dust, which flakes off and mixes with the fuel and iron, thus clogging the cupola by making slag or dirty metal.

30. Cost of Materials for Daubing.—Fireclay is the best material for daubing, but many founders consider it too costly; but if one takes into consideration the extra amount of slag and the cost of relining the cupola every few months made necessary by the use of a cheap daubing, they will perceive that cheap daubings are the most expensive in the end. In putting on daubings, the smaller the amount used, as a rule, the better. The daubing should rarely be allowed to exceed 1 inch in thickness at any part, as shown at *b*, Fig. 7; this is far better than having the whole melting portion filled out to the level of the cupola lining at the edges of the zone. Many cupola tenders think it necessary to fill out the melting zone even with the rest of the lining. If it is considered that heavy bodies of thick clay cannot be dried thoroughly by a whole day's firing, and that only the surface of the daubing is dried before the blast is put on, it is evident that it is not proper to use thick daubings. In case the lining burns out badly in spots, pieces of firebrick embedded in clay may be used to fill it in, but a lump of wet clay should never be employed, as it is likely to come away from the lining as soon as the blast is started, or in a short time afterwards.

31. Badly Burned Melting Zones.—When the melting zone becomes burned out so badly as to enlarge it 4 inches or more beyond the general lining, thus permitting the blast to escape between the charge and the lining, it should be

repaired in a substantial manner, and its diameter reduced
to a dimension not more than 5 inches greater than the
diameter of the lining above the melting point. This can
often be accomplished by taking split firebricks, about
2 inches thick, shown in Fig. 5 (*a*) and (*b*), which can be
obtained of firebrick manufacturers, or may be made by
splitting the whole bricks, and bedding them firmly in good
clay against the solid lining, thus bringing the melting zone
to approximately the form shown at *v*, Fig. 2.

CUPOLA BOTTOMS.

32. Bottom Props. — When the cupola has been
daubed, the bottom doors *d, d*, shown in Fig. 2, are lifted
up and a prop *y* is placed under them. The doors for cupolas
having an inside diameter not greater that 40 inches can be
held with one prop, but over this size it is best to have two
props. These props are best made of wrought iron, and
range in size from 1½ to 3 inches in diameter. It is very
important to have a solid foundation under the props, for
if there is the least settling of the drop doors after the
cupola commences to melt, the iron is apt to break out at
the joint of the doors and probably injure the men and
cause a loss of a heat and some iron.

33. Foundation for Props. — The foundations under
the props may be made of solid iron blocks *u*, as shown in
Fig. 2, ranging from 3 to 5 inches in thickness and from
12 to 24 inches square, according to the diameter and
height of the cupola. Where the cupola is over 50 inches
inside diameter, it is well to have a stone or brick foundation under the plate. In putting up the props, they should
be so placed that the supporting columns of the cupola will
not be in the way when it is necessary to knock the props
down in order to drop the bottom at the close of the heat.
After the doors are propped up, it is a good plan to close
up all the joints on the inside with soft clay, rubbed in
tightly, as this may prevent the bottom sand, when dried,
from running out and leaving a hole through which the

metal may run.   If there should be small holes in the bottom, caused by former leakage, they should be covered solidly with a piece of plate iron bedded into clay.

34. Quality of Material Used in Bottoms.—The bottom of a cupola is formed of sand, as shown in Figs. 2 and 7. The conditions require a sand that cannot bake so hard as not to drop readily when the doors are opened; the sand must also be of such a character that it cannot be washed away by the action of the blast and the molten metal flowing out of the tap hole. The sand generally used for this purpose is obtained from the gangways in light workshops and the dump-dirt piles of large workshops. This sand is mixed with what may be saved from the cupola bottom of the previous heat. Should this mixture be too weak, clay wash or new molding sand may be mixed with it. It is very important to have the bottom sand of the right strength and dampness, for if it is too strong or too damp, it may give trouble during the heat or when the doors are dropped, and if too weak or too dry, it is apt to be cut away by the flow of the metal or the force of the blast.

35. Preparing the Sand for Cupola Bottoms. The sand having been well mixed and made of the same consistency or temper as green sand for molding purposes, is then passed through a ½-inch riddle, after which it is shoveled on to the bottom either by passing it through the breast hole *c*, Fig. 7, or through the bottom by having but half of the bottom door in place, or by letting it down from the charging door.   When the sand is all in, the cupola man goes inside and spreads it, giving it a proper slope ; it is then rammed down firmly with the butt end of a rammer to a hardness similar to that necessary in ramming the nowel of a flat plate casting.

36. Density and Slope of a Sand Bottom. — If the sand is rammed too hard, it may cause the iron to boil when it commences to gather over the bottom, and if too soft, it may be cut by the wash of the metal or force of the blast.   After the sand has been rammed, the hand or a

board is used to give it a gradual incline from the back to
the front of the cupola, leaving the outer edges higher than
the bottom.   If the bed is not given an even slope, the
hollows or depressions will retain metal, which may make
dull iron and cause a waste of metal when the bottom is
dropped.   When the sand is weak, the bottom may be
lightly sprinkled with water from a brush to cause a hard
crust to form on the surface of the bed when heated ;
but care must be taken to use no more than will merely
dampen the surface, since if the water goes any deeper it
may cause the iron to boil and blow on the bottom, thus
resulting in injury to the bottom.   The slope given to the
bed is very important, and varies, according to conditions,
from $\frac{1}{2}$ to 1 inch per foot. When the cupola is a slow melter,
or when irons are used that solidify quickly, it is advisable
to adopt the steepest slope, for the reason that it causes the
iron to collect quickly at the breast in a hotter state than if
it had to dribble slowly over the bed before reaching it.
While this is true, the slope should not be made any steeper
than necessary, since the steeper the slope is made, the
swifter the metal rushes out of the tap hole, making it difficult to stop up.   In finishing up the bottom, it is a good
plan to dig out a little sand back of the tap hole and replace
the regular bottom sand with some good strong new loam
sand or clay.   This will serve as an aid to prevent the action
of the tapping bar from cutting up the bottom immediately
inside the tapping hole.

MAKING THE BREAST, TAP HOLE, AND SPOUT.

**37. Dimensions of the Breast, Tap Hole, and
Spout.**—The hole for forming the breast or front, shown
at c, Fig. 7, is generally about 6 inches wide by 8 inches
high, and is left open to give draft to the cupola until the
fire is well started.   When all is ready to put in the front,
the breast hole is brushed out clean on the bottom and is
slightly wetted with clay water, after which a handful of
wet clay is rubbed on the bottom and a $\frac{3}{4}$-inch to $1\frac{1}{2}$-inch

rod n, shown in Fig. 2, is bedded into the clay on the level of the bottom. Pieces of coke 3 or 4 inches long are coated with clay and placed about the stick n until the breast hole is completely and solidly filled, after which the stick n is withdrawn and the face of the breast and the tap hole dressed with clay. The coke expands when heated and forms a tight and durable breast. Sometimes the breast is made by fitting a piece of board in the breast hole flush with the inside of the cupola lining, and then ramming clay into the hole against the outside of the board and around a stick. After the breast has been filled, the front is cut away so as to reduce its thickness at the tap hole, as shown at d, Fig. 7. This is done to make the length of the tapping hole as short as possible, since a long tapping hole causes the metal to chill in it, which may cause trouble during the first tapping and often during the whole heat. In cutting out the breast to shorten the tapping hole, the slope from the face of the cupola to the tap hole should be gradual, as a very abrupt slope adds to the difficulty in tapping and stopping.

38. Materials Used in Making the Breast.—The material used in forming the breast should be of as refractory a character as possible, the best material being a mixture of fine clay and sharp sand, such as used in daubing the melting zone of the cupola; the next in order of value are good grades of blue or yellow clays. Some melters try to make the breast with molding sand wetted

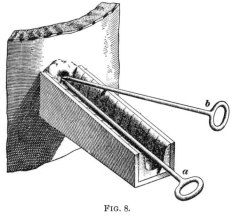

FIG. 8.

with clay, but this material is likely to give trouble, especially in long heats. In lining the cupola spout shown in

Fig. 8, the same material may be used as for making the breast. After the bieast and spout are formed, the rod *n*, shown in Fig. 2, for forming the tap hole is pulled out, and some live coals are shoveled in the spout and against the breast to assist in drying them. This is continued up to the time the blast is put on, the heat of which is generally sufficient to leave the tapping hole in fair shape for its work; but where it can be done, it is best to let the iron run from 5 to 20 minutes before stopping up. This can be done best in large cupolas that have large ladles for taking away the metal.

39. Use of Clay Cores for Tap Holes.—Some founders place clay cores that have been dried in an oven, and have a tap hole formed in them, in the breast of the cupola. These are kept on hand, and when placed in the breast holes, clay is rammed around them. This plan works very well, since it insures a dry hole for the metal to run through. Where the metal runs steadily out of a tap hole, a smaller hole can be used than where it has to be let out at intervals. When it is necessary to stop it up every now and then, the hole should not be larger than is actually necessary, since the larger the hole, the more difficult it is to stop it up. In forming the spout, its bottom should be made small in diameter, not to exceed 4 inches; for when made wide, it causes the metal to spread, and then the metal not only becomes dull, but has a tendency to wash over the sides of the spout. If this latter accident should happen, the iron may be thrown by the moist sand in such a way as to injure the men in front of the cupola, or it may cause the loss of considerable metal.

CHARGING CUPOLAS.

40. Starting the Fire in a Cupola.—In building a fire in a cupola, some light combustible, such as dry shavings, oiled waste, charcoal, or straw, is passed through the charging door to the bottom of the cupola. On top of this, dry soft kindling wood is placed in such a manner as to catch fire readily, and over this, heavier wood is placed. The amount of wood required will depend on its character and that of the coke or coal used. All that is necessary is to have sufficient wood to set the coke or coal burning rapidly, and any more than this only fills up the cupola with ashes and prevents the coke or coal settling down in such a manner as to give proper support to the iron when it is charged. Care is necessary in selecting the kindling wood to have it well dried and of as soft a quality as possible. The coke or coal should be of medium size, as too small a fuel will choke the fire and too large lumps will require too much kindling, besides taking too long to get the fire kindled.

41. Charging the Fuel in a Cupola.—In charging the fuel, about one-half the amount required for the bed is first put on before the fire is started. When this burns up brightly, one-half of the remaining portion of the fuel is shoveled in, and when this is fairly under way, the rest is charged. As soon as the fuel burns up evenly, it is ready for charging the iron; but before this is done, it should be remembered that the bed of fuel must be thoroughly afire all around the sides, as any neglect of this may cause the cupola to give poor results all through the heat. It is not uncommon to have ladles choked up, castings lost, or the bottom of the cupola dropped before the heat is finished, simply because the bed of fuel was not thoroughly afire before starting to charge the iron. The time required to kindle the fire to get it in good condition for charging the iron generally ranges from 2 to 3 hours in large cupolas. Coal requires a longer time than coke, and wet fuel a longer time than dry. It is bad policy to let the bed burn longer than is necessary to get it well started, as this only results in a loss of fuel.

42. Use of Blast.—Some founders arrange to have the cupola charged and the blast on in from 1 to 2 hours after first starting the fire. This necessitates the use of a light blast on the fuel to hurry the fire. This should not be done if it can be avoided, as the bed ought to kindle gradually of itself, with merely the draft that the open breast and tuyeres give it; these can be closed should the fire burn too rapidly. Letting the fire burn with natural draft and occupying 2 or 3 hours in burning up ready for charging affords time to bring the walls of the cupola to a temperature agreeing more nearly with that of the fire, and is a factor that is not only beneficial to the lining, but also aids in giving better results in taking off the heat. Those that have a uniform, well-kindled fire before charging the iron, combined with a good breast and tap hole, will have the least difficulty in running off a successful heat.

43. Amount of Charge.—The first considerations that present themselves in commencing to charge a cupola are: How much fuel should be used on the bed, how much between the charges of iron, and what weight of iron should be in the charges. The amount of fuel in the bed depends largely on the height of the lower tuyeres. With anthracite coal it will require a height of from 12 to 16 inches above the top of the lower tuyeres. With coke, a height of from 18 to 24 inches is required; which means in both cases a bed of solid fuel well ignited before commencing to charge the iron. In weight, it requires from 10 to 20 per cent. more of hard coal than good coke. The specific gravity of coke being less than coal, a given weight of it will stand higher above the tuyeres, but coal will sustain a heavier burden than coke, due to its being a more solid, dense fuel. Hardwood charcoal and gas-house coke have been used for melting iron; the ratios being about 1 of charcoal to 3 of iron, and 1 of gas-house coke to 4 of iron. Of recent years these fuels are little used.

44. Influence of Height of Tuyeres on Weight of Charge.—Owing to the great variation in the height of the tuyeres, it is impossible to lay down any fast rules that can be applied to determine the weight of the first charge of iron in reference to the weight of fuel in the bed. Again, the ratio of iron to fuel depends on the character of the iron used; thus, a greater weight of light pig or scrap can be used than if heavier pieces of iron were charged. The following will give an idea of the weight of iron to charge: Starting with a 20-inch cupola, charge 300 pounds of iron on the bed; then, for every increase of 2 inches in the internal diameter of a cupola, add 300 pounds of iron on the bed. This will give a 30-inch cupola a first charge of iron weighing 1,800 pounds; a 40-inch cupola, 3,300 pounds; a 50-inch cupola, 4,800 pounds; a 60-inch cupola, 6,300 pounds; a 70-inch cupola, 7,800 pounds, and an 80-inch cupola, 9,300 pounds. These weights may often be increased from 10 to 30 per cent., but it is best to start with the figures given above and gradually increase the burden until the best weights are ascertained by actual tests. As a rule, the weight of the iron charged on the bed is heavier than that in the succeeding charges, although, where a uniform mixture is used throughout the heat, some founders make all succeeding charges equal in weight to that of the first charge.

45. Amount of Fuel Between Charges of Iron. The next consideration is how much fuel is it necessary to place between each of the succeeding charges of iron. As an approximation, it can be said that the amount of fuel between charges should average about 10 per cent. of the weight of the charges of iron, a little more coal being required than coke. The idea involved in placing fuel between the charges of iron is to keep the height of the bed by means of the descending fuel up to the thickness existing when the first iron commences to melt. In watching this point carefully, the melter may be able in some cases to do with less than 10 per cent. of fuel between the charges. In ascertaining the percentage of fuel used to melt the iron, all the fuel consumed in the bed, as well as that used between the charges of iron, must be considered.

46. Ratios of Fuel to Iron.—If 5 tons of fuel melt 50 tons of iron, the melting ratio is one of fuel to 10 of iron, which is about as small a ratio of fuel as can be used to get good hot iron; and to get this ratio, the best conditions must prevail. It is rarely wise to be sparing in the use of fuel, as the least mishap, by uneven charging or from an unsteady blast, may result in giving dull iron, causing a loss in bunged-up ladles and bad castings at one heat that may more than balance the cost of fuel that could be saved during a month's melting.

The general average of cupola practice is to use ratios of from 1 to 6 up to 1 to 8 with good coke, and from 1 to 5 up to 1 to 7 with hard coal, the former being required to melt iron for light work, or that requiring hot iron, and the latter for heavy castings, or where the work does not require the hottest metal. In charging fuel and iron, they should be weighed, so that the amount of material being used may be known. Too many founders charge the fuel and iron by guesswork, but uniform results cannot be expected from this practice. Each pile of iron or scrap as it is brought to be charged should be weighed and a record kept of what goes into the cupola; and the same should be done with all the fuel and flux that may be used. The fuel is weighed either before coming on the staging to be charged into the cupola by a fork or shovel, or else it is measured in barrels or baskets and dumped from them into the cupola. Whatever way it is done, the exact quantity being used should be known definitely.

47. Effects From Too Much or Too Little Fuel. If too little fuel is placed between the charges of iron, the bed as it is consumed will finally lower itself to the level of the lower tuyeres. The nearer the bed approaches this level, thus falling below the proper height, the more dull the iron becomes, and eventually it results in stopping the iron from melting. If too much fuel is placed between the charges, it will raise the bed above the proper height and the iron above the melting zone, which results in causing slow melting, and may finally stop the melting until the bed burns down to the proper height, but a high bed will produce hotter iron than a low bed. The best height at which to maintain the level of the bed varies with different cupolas, and is regulated by the area and form of the tuyeres and their connections, as well as by the pressure of the blast. If the size, form, etc., of the tuyeres and their connections are fixed, the height of the bed may be varied by changing the pressure of the blast; the greater the pressure, the higher the point at which the melting takes place.

48. Indication of Correct Charging.—Whether a cupola is being handled to the best advantage or not is shown by the fluidity of the metal and the speed of melting. The fluidity of the metal and the speed of melting are regulated in accordance with the indications by varying the weight of the charges of iron. If the iron becomes duller near the latter end of the charge than it was at the first, it is evidence that the charge of iron is too heavy, and if such heavy charges of iron are continued, the result will be dull iron for the balance of the heat. If the iron comes down hot, with an increase of speed in melting at the end of each charge, it is evidence that the charges of iron are too light or the charges of fuel too great. It must be understood that these conditions hold even though the proper height of the bed of fuel is maintained in the melting zone by the descending charges of fuel. When the best weight of charge is known and used, the speed of melting, as well as the degree of fluidity of the metal, will be uniform. Where the cupolas are run continuously without tapping or stopping up, variations in the weight of the charge will produce the greatest changes in the fluidity of the metal.

49. Methods for Charging Heavy and Light Irons.—The charging of fuel and iron is generally done by hand. In throwing pig iron into a cupola, it is best to place the ends toward the lining as much as possible, though it is of much greater importance to have the charges level. For cupolas under 50 inches and over 30 inches inside diameter, it is necessary to have the pigs broken into two pieces, and for cupolas under 30 inches, the pigs should be broken into three pieces. When the pigs are long in proportion to the diameter of the cupola, they are very apt to wedge themselves in such a way as to hold up the charge, and, consequently, do not permit the even and systematic charging necessary to economical use of the fuel and good melting.   In charging iron, it should be dropped as gently as possible on the top of the bed, since throwing it in carelessly may cause it to injure the lining, thus creating slag; or it may embed itself in the fuel in such a manner that it disturbs the regularity of the charging.   The iron should be charged as closely together as possible, in order to prevent the escape of heat up the stack.

The largest pieces of iron should be placed on the fuel and the smallest on top; the pieces will then melt simultaneously and so come down together and give a more uniform mixture. This is true in making mixtures of pig iron and scrap, as well as mixtures made with pig iron only.   The heavier the iron used, whether pig iron or scrap, the more fuel will be required and the slower it will melt.   When very large pieces of scrap are to be melted, they should be put in the second or third charge according to the size of the cupola, for if very heavy lumps are placed on the bed, they are liable to sink to the level of the lower tuyeres or even to the spout, before being melted; they may even clog up the cupola and stop the progress of the melting.

50.   Charging Different Grades of Iron.—It often happens that founders are called on to make castings of several different grades or brands of iron at one heat.   Some of the castings may be made of very soft iron, while others will require hard iron.   In such cases it is best to endeavor to place a charge of medium-grade iron between the charge having the soft iron and that having the hard iron.   Then, if some of the medium-grade iron does melt down and mix with either of the extremes, it will not result in as much harm as if the extremes had melted together.   If they show a tendency to mix, it is well to separate the charges farther apart by introducing a thick charge of fuel, so that the first one will all melt down before the second charge reaches the melting point.   If there is doubt of this method not working successfully, the special grade may be melted down by itself without any mixture, and when all this has come down, the blast may be shut off and the bed recharged with fuel to the original height; the next extreme of iron may then be charged and the melting proceeded with in the usual manner. Both of these methods will require much more fuel than is needed for a uniform grade of iron throughout the heat; but they are convenient for achieving special results. Whatever method may be employed in charging, the feature to be observed is to always exercise the greatest care to charge both fuel and iron in as even a manner as possible.

51. Irregular Charging.—When more fuel is placed on one side than on the other, or when the iron is not level at the end of the charge, very unsatisfactory results may be expected. Irregular charging may not only cause dull iron, but also result in clogging up the cupola to such an extent as to stop the process of melting entirely. After a cupola is once filled to the charging door, it should be kept full until all the iron for that heat is charged, for by keeping the cupola full it not only utilizes the heat better, but also keeps the gases and flame from affecting the men doing the charging.

SLAGGING A CUPOLA AND FLUXES USED.

52. Principle of Fluxes.—Where heats are of long duration, or where dirty or burned iron is used, it is necessary to use a *flux*, and to make special provisions for the slag by means of fluxes. The **fluxes** are materials that are lighter than iron, and that when melted in a cupola will float on the liquid iron and absorb and liquefy the non-metallic residue of the iron and the ash of the fuel, so that these may be discharged from the cupola through a slag hole q, shown in Fig. 2. When this refuse remains in the cupola, it soon becomes so great in bulk as to fill up much of the space required for the fuel. The longer the heats or the dirtier the iron, the more fluxing and slagging out are required.

53. Importance of Fluxes and Slagging.—A great many foundries have fine floor scrap, *shot iron* from tumbling barrels, and gates with the sand on, which, when charged with other iron into the cupola, create more or less residue that, if not carried off, will remain in the cupola and clog it up rapidly. Where such materials have to be charged with the regular grade of scrap and pig iron, the cupola will need to be slagged out more frequently. The capacity of a cupola is so greatly increased by fluxing and slagging that some cupolas, which could not otherwise be run for over three or four hours, can be kept in blast day and night for a whole week when properly slagged.

54. Kinds of Fluxes.—The substance used as a flux usually consists of a carbonate of lime, which is found in the form of limestone, oyster shells, clam shells, calcite, chalk, marble spalls, and dolomite; spar, fluorspar, feldspar, and magnesia are also used for fluxes. The weight of flux necessary is dependent on the character of the iron and fuel, also on the kind of the flux used. With limestone, the richer it is in lime, the less there will be required. The weight of limestone required to make a fluid slag may range from 50 to 80 pounds per ton of iron charged. Where the scrap is cleaned, and sandless pig iron and a good class of fuel are used, so as to leave a low percentage of residue, 30 to 50 pounds of good limestone per ton of metal may be sufficient to make a fluid slag. It is generally necessary to experiment with the flux in order to ascertain the best percentage to use.

Marble spalls are chippings from marble quarries, and are, as a rule, of purer limestone than the other forms. The amount required is nearly the same as that of limestone. Fluorspar is a most excellent flux and surpasses limestone, shells, or marble in producing a good slag, and also does not change the character of the iron. The objection to fluorspar is its cost, especially to those foundries situated at a distance from the mines. Fluorspar is sometimes mixed with other fluxes. Some foundrymen claim that fluorspar attacks the lining and hastens its destruction.

55. Composition of Limestone Fluxes.—The elements of the slag combine with the oxide of silica that comes from the oxidation of the silicon in the iron, and also combine with the oxide of manganese that comes from the manganese in the iron, and which, if very high in quantity in the iron, will carry off considerable sulphur from the fuel into the slag. In Table I is shown the composition of three samples of limestone fluxes. Those shown in columns 2 and 3 are the best, because of their freedom from sulphur. The limestone given in column 1 is very hard and of a dark color, and is a grade chiefly used for blast furnaces, although it also works well in cupolas. It is obtained at Newcastle, Pa.

TABLE I.

COMPOSITION OF LIMESTONES.

	1.	2.	3.
Silica	3.00	1.980	.54
Iron oxide	.92	.600	.12
Alumina	1.25	.900	.36
Phosphorus	.02	.037	
Sulphur	.02		
Carbonate of lime	92.10	82.850	98.78
Carbonate of magnesia	1.26	13.040	
Lime oxide	51.57	46.410	55.32
Magnesia oxide	1.63	17.230	

56. Charging the Flux.—The charging of limestone or any other flux is generally done by placing it on top of the iron, although it is often charged on top of the fuel or mixed with the iron and fuel; placing it on the iron is generally the best plan, since it then leaves the fuel more compact and in better form to sustain the iron. In using limestone, it should be broken into small pieces about the size of eggs, and should then be spread evenly over the charge;

oyster shells or clam shells are used without breaking, and the weight of shells required is about the same as that of limestone. When shells are first charged, they make a crackling noise and throw off flakes that cause some waste, but not sufficient to be excessive. The limestone given in column 2 is of a much softer quality than that in column 1, and is also more white and clear. It is known as Kelly Island limestone, and is mined at Kelly Island, Ohio. Column 3 gives the analysis of a grade that is softer and purer than either of the others, and has somewhat the appearance of marble. It is called calcite, and is obtained from the Benson mines, New York.

57. Quantity of Flux.—Whether the flux used is sufficient in quantity or not is generally shown by the fluidity of the slag, which should be as fluid as practicable. If it does not run freely, it is due to one of two causes: Either the cupola is running cold on account of poor combustion, or else there is not sufficient flux being used. A very great excess of limestone flux will also make a dull slag. When the slag is not sufficiently fluid, it runs out so sluggishly that it is very liable to pile up in the cupola to the level of the tuyeres. If this occurs, the cold blast will chill the slag, clogging the tuyeres, and the melting will be retarded or stopped entirely.

58. Necessity of a Free Slag.—It is very important to obtain a good free slag, i. e., one that is fluid, so as to prevent it piling up any higher than the slag hole. If the slag does pile up, the cupola would be far better off if no flux had been used, as its use only increases the amount of material that must be removed in order to successfully continue melting. In fact, if a cupola can be made to run free and clean to the end of the heat without using a flux, it is only a waste of money to use it, since, besides the cost of the flux itself, it also requires some fuel to melt it. Furthermore, it increases the loss of iron, as slag contains 3 to 6 per cent. of iron chemically combined with it, and also carries off small particles of iron that are mechanically mixed with it. Besides, it costs considerable to haul away the slag from the cupola and the yard, for, as a rule, 20 to 70 pounds of slag are created per ton of iron melted when using a flux.

59. Methods of Slagging.—When cupolas require slagging out, the flux is not to be charged until the cupola is filled to the level of the charging door, or until it has been melting for about ½ hour. In slagging out a cupola, some cupola tenders open the slag hole as soon as they think there is any accumulation of slag, and leave it open during the remainder of the heat, while others will close it after every tapping, leaving it closed until the melted iron brings the slag again up to the slag hole. The latter method is largely a matter of guesswork, and if the slag should rise above the slag hole to the level of the tuyeres, it may do much injury. It is a much safer plan to leave the slag hole open after it has been tapped. In either case, the slag hole will require watching; for, should any lump of fuel or chilled slag become fast in it, the slag might rise to the level of the tuyeres. If the slag is running thin and hot, the danger from it is less than if it were thick and sluggish.

FUEL COMBUSTION IN CUPOLAS.

60. The Blast.—In order to melt iron rapidly, it is necessary to force air into the cupola. This forced air is called the **blast.** It is claimed that 30,000 cubic feet of air, measured at atmospheric pressure and 62° F., is consumed in melting a ton of iron. This amount of air weighs 400 pounds more than the ton of iron that it assists to melt. Air consists chiefly of two gases, nitrogen and oxygen, which have the weight and volume given in Table II. The column headed Volume gives the percentage of each element in the air by volume, and the column headed Weight gives the percentage of each element by weight. One cubic foot of air at 32° F., and at the pressure of the air at the sea level, weighs .08 pound.

TABLE II.

COMPOSITION OF AIR.

	Volume.	Weight.
Nitrogen.................	79.19	76.99
Oxygen	20.81	23.01
Total	100.00	100.00

61. Combustion.—The oxygen of the air, when combined with the carbon of the fuel, creates **combustion.** The nitrogen does not aid combustion, but is an inert gas that dilutes the oxygen and carries off some of the heat. It requires 2 atoms of oxygen to produce the complete combustion of 1 atom of carbon. When the hot carbon combines with the oxygen of the blast entering the cupola, the result is perfect combustion, if the above proportion be steadily maintained; but this is not practicable in a cupola.

62. Heat from the Combustion of Carbon.—Since oxygen and carbon are the chief factors necessary to support combustion, it is important to note their influence in obtaining *perfect* combustion. One pound of carbon combined with the necessary oxygen to form carbonic-acid gas, which consists of 1 part of carbon, C, and 2 parts of oxygen, O_2, or CO_2, develops 14,500 units of heat. The specific heat of cast iron is about .13, and the average melting point may be taken as 2,200° F. If foundry coke containing 86.96 per cent. carbon, as shown in Table V, be used, then the theoretical amount necessary to heat 1 ton of cast iron (2,240 lb.) from 60° F. to 2,200° F., not allowing for any losses, is

$$\frac{(2,200 - 60) \times 2,240 \times .13}{14,500 \times .8696} = 49.5 \text{ pounds of coke.}$$

One pound of carbon burned to carbonic oxide, which consists of 1 atom of carbon, C, and 1 atom of oxygen, O, or CO, gives out only 4,400 heat units. The amount of coke under these conditions necessary to melt 1 ton of iron is

$$\frac{(2,200 - 60) \times 2,240 \times .13}{4,400 \times .8696} = 163.1 \text{ pounds.}$$

As a matter of fact neither of these conditions prevails alone. The combination of the carbon with the oxygen of the blast produces carbonic-acid gas, CO_2, at a point a little above the tuyeres, and this gas in passing up through the fuel heated to incandescence takes up more carbon and is converted into carbonic-oxide gas. This will again change to carbonic-acid gas if more air is admitted to it. The analysis of the escaping gases shows that about one-half of the carbon goes off as carbonic oxide and is incompletely burned. It must also be remembered that additional heat is necessary to melt the iron after it is raised to a temperature of $2,200°$ F. and that neither of the above calculations takes into account the latent heat of fusion of iron. As the calculations are only intended to compare the two conditions of combustion, this will not make any difference. This extra heat does not increase the temperature of the iron, but its energy is used in changing it from a solid to a liquid state. Clement's experiments show that it requires over 500 heat units to raise the temperature of 1 pound of cast iron from $62°$ F. to the melting point and to continue the heat until the molten condition is reached. The amount of coke for complete melting in the theoretical furnace is $\dfrac{2,240 \times 500}{14,500 \times .8696} = 89$ pounds when the carbon is burned to carbonic-acid gas, and 294 pounds when burned only to carbonic oxide.

Allowances must be made for various losses. Generally they are as much as 10 per cent. for moisture in the coke, 10 per cent. for radiation of heat through the lining, and 20 per cent. for loss of heat from the top of the cupola, or fully 40 per cent. in all; so that in practice most founders consider the melting of 1 ton of iron with 200 pounds of fuel, or a ratio of 1 to 10, as good work.

63. Pressure and Volume of Blast. — The best pressure and volume of blast for cupola work are largely dependent on the character of the fuel used. Coal requires a pressure from one-fourth to one-third greater than coke, owing to its being a more dense fuel. The volume of air that each fuel consumes is about the same. The necessity of a greater pressure for coal than for coke results in a greater loss of heat when using coal. It is desirable that the blast be as strong and the volume of air blown into the cupola be as great as can be utilized to good advantage. However, too great a blast pressure only serves to cut out the lining of the cupola and reduces the fluidity of the metal.

TABLE III.

PRESSURES AND VOLUMES OF AIR FOR CUPOLAS.

Inside Diameter of Cupola. Inches.	Melting Capacity Per Hour. Pounds.	Cubic Feet of Air Per Minute.	Pressure in Ounces of Blast.
22	1,200	324	5
26	1,900	507	6
30	2,880	768	7
35	4,130	1,102	8
40	6,178	1,646	10
46	8,900	2,375	12
53	12,500	3,353	14
60	16,560	4,416	14
72	23,800	6,364	16
84	33,300	8,880	16

64. Blast Gauges.—Sometimes cupolas are equipped with **blast gauges** for the purpose of measuring the pressure of the blast. This is a very good plan for cupolas in which the tuyeres are kept open; but when this is not done, a blast gauge is not of much value in showing the amount of air that enters the cupola. This is due to the fact that if the tuyeres become stopped up, it causes a greater pressure of the air in the outer pipes than exists in the interior of the cupola. By observing the speed of the blower, the rate of melting, and the force of the blast at the charging door, a knowledge of the volume and pressure of the air being utilized in the cupola can be obtained. The volumes and pressures of air for cupolas ranging from 22 to 84 inches in diameter, and their melting capacities per hour, are given in Table III, which is compiled from the results of numerous tests made by a prominent manufacturing company.

TAPPING OUT A CUPOLA.

65. Precautions Necessary in Tapping.—Tapping is, as a rule, the most hazardous part of cupola work, for if a cupola tender does not understand his business, or goes about the work carelessly, he is very liable to be burned. The tools used for tapping consist of round bars of iron or steel ranging from $\frac{5}{8}$ to 1 inch in diameter, and from 3 to 12 feet in length. The longer bars are generally used where the ladles are placed under the spout in such a manner as to prevent the cupola tender from standing near the tap hole. Where the conditions permit the tender to stand near the spout, bars 3 to 5 feet long are used. Tapping bars should be pointed at one end, so that they can easily pick out any obstruction in the tap hole.

66. Tools for Tapping.—It is well to have three or four tapping bars constantly on hand, for at any time the

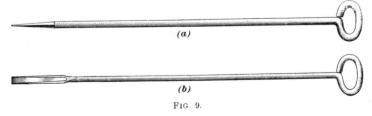

(a)

(b)

Fig. 9.

metal may come rushing out against the point of the bar, even before the hole is fully opened, and burn away the point of the bar and greatly injure its utility. A pointed tapping bar is shown in Fig. 9 (*a*), and a chisel bar at (*b*). If the tender finds himself without bars to complete the tapping, the iron may run into the tuyeres and cause great damage before he can find a suitable bar. Some of the extra bars should be made of steel, having their points of a chisel shape and well tempered, as there are times when a tap hole may clog up so firmly that it will require good pointed bars and a sledge to open it.

67. Method of Tapping.—In tapping, the bar should never be driven straight into the center of the tap hole after the manner shown at *a*, Fig. 8. This only wedges the bar and makes the tapping more difficult, and often requires a sledge to drive the bar inwards; this method may do once or twice during the heat, but if repeated continually soon breaks up the breast so as to give trouble in stopping. The proper way to tap out is to dig out the old stopping plug, or *bod*, by picking around the outer edge of the tapping hole, applying the tapping bar in the manner shown at *b*, Fig. 8. By working the bar around the outer edge of the stopping bod, it is soon loosened, until the pressure of the metal is about to burst the bod outwards. When this is done, the points of the tapping bar can be easily inserted at one side of the hole to pry the daubing clear of any support and leave a clean hole for the free flow of the metal. As soon as the bar has started the metal freely, its point should be dipped in a pail of water to cool and reharden it. By such treatment as this, a bar is kept in good form ready for the next tap. The tender should always have a stand or place in which to keep his tapping tools and stopping tools, clay, and water pail, so that they will be at hand the instant they are needed.

***

STOPPING A CUPOLA.

68. Tools for Stopping.—The tools used for stopping up the tap hole when metal is running out of it consist of long bod sticks or rods as shown at (*a*) and (*b*), Fig. 10. The iron stopper or bod stick, shown at Fig. 10 (*a*), may range from $\frac{5}{8}$ to 1 inch in diameter, and may be from 4 to 12 feet long. The wooden bod stick having an iron end *a*, as shown at (*b*), is most convenient where long bod sticks are necessary. Some tenders use an all-wood bod stick, ranging from $1\frac{1}{4}$ to 2 inches in diameter. These are objectionable, for when the stopping bod falls off, which is a common

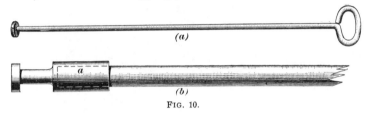

FIG. 10.

occurrence, without the cupola tender noticing it, the act of shoving the bare end of the wooden bod stick into the flowing metal will cause the iron to fly in all directions, and may result in badly burning any one standing near the cupola spout. Of the two forms of bod sticks, the iron one is preferable, but on account of its not being as convenient to handle as the wooden ones, it is not so generally used.

69. Stopping a Cupola Before and After Tapping.—When stopping up the tap hole against the stream of outflowing metal, it is better not to push the stopping rod directly against the flowing metal in an effort to strike the hole. Such a method causes the iron to be divided by the stopping stick and results in more or less of it being thrown out of the spout on the floor, where it will be spattered in all directions; it may also wash the stopping clay from the end of the bar. The proper way is to hold the stopping bod above the stream, and when near the stopping hole to push it down obliquely, which brings the bar at a sharp angle with the stream and permits the hole to be stopped in a firm manner without causing any spattering of the metal.

70. Materials for Stopping a Cupola.—The materials used for making stopping clays or bods, where the cupola is tapped at short intervals, should be of as friable and dry a nature as practicable. In such a case there is little or no pressure in the cupola to shove out the bods, and all that is required is sufficient tenacity in the stopping clay to hold back the blast and a head-pressure of 1 or 2 inches of iron. Having the stopping bods friable and dry will make tapping easy and prevent that spattering and boiling of the iron at the tap hole that strong, close, wet bods may cause. For cupolas that are tapped at from 15 to 20 minute intervals, the stopping mixture should be stronger, in order that it may adhere to the sides of the tapping hole sufficiently to hold back the pressure of the metal. With a longer time between taps, the stopping mixture may be stronger without causing blowing, as there is more time to dry it. In making mixtures for short-interval tapping, new molding or loam sand mixed with about one-third of fireclay works very well; or the molding sand may be used by itself, having been wetted with thick clay wash. Bod mixtures for use where there are long intervals between taps generally require to be made almost entirely of clay, mixing from one-quarter to one-third of sea coal, blackening, or saw dust with the clay. In mixing the stopping clays, they should be made quite stiff, for if too soft, the mixture cannot be made to stay in place.

_____

CAPACITY OF A CUPOLA.

71. Influence of Slagging on the Capacity of a Cupola.—The amount of iron that a cupola will melt cannot be given very readily. Some founders can keep a cupola in blast and doing good, clean melting, by slagging out, for a whole week; whereas, if it were not slagged out, it would clog up in a few hours. The approximate amount of clean iron cupolas should melt with good fuel, and still have a clean drop when not slagged out, is given in Table IV. When founders desire to complete their heats in from 1 to 2 hours, the latter being about the longest time a cupola should run without slagging, Table IV will aid them in selecting the proper size of cupola.

TABLE IV.

MELTING CAPACITY OF CUPOLAS.

Inside Diameter of Cupola. Inches.	Melting Capacity When Not Slagging Out. Tons.
20	2
25	3
30	5
35	7
40	10
45	12
50	15
55	20
60	25
65	30
70	35
75	40
80	50

72. Comparison of Sizes of Cupolas. — If, with one of the larger sizes of cupolas given in Table IV, the equipment of a shop or the force of employes is not sufficient to carry the iron away from the cupola as fast as it melts, and the weights of the heats are in keeping with the capacity of the cupola as shown in the table, then a smaller cupola should be used. To get the tonnage out of it, it is necessary to slag it out and to allow more time for pouring off. This can be carried to such extremes that a cupola over 30 inches in diameter can, by having upper tuyeres, be run for 10 hours or more, requiring but a few men to take care of the iron. There is really no economy in running very long heats. The cupola should be of such a capacity that it will melt iron as fast as it can be handled. Where small cupolas are used for long heats the molders stand around waiting for iron when they should be at work molding.

COKE AND COAL IN MELTING.

73. Comparison of Qualities of Coke and Coal.
The value of coke as a fuel for melting iron was first successfully demonstrated in 1860 by the Clinton furnace, of
Pittsburg, Pa. Since that time its use has so increased
that now very few furnaces use coal entirely. The advantage of coke over anthracite coal is that it requires less
blast and melts the iron more quickly than coal; and generally it is a much cheaper fuel and requires less time to
kindle it, but often burns too fast. For this reason, coal
excels coke for melting massive pieces of scrap and for pro-
longing heats beyond the time possible with coke, unless
slagging out is practiced. Pieces of scrap weighing as much
as 6,000 pounds have been melted by the use of coal in a
45-inch cupola.

In charging heavy pieces of iron, the bed of fuel must
always be raised higher than is done for ordinary charging
of medium pig and scrap. When a founder has difficulty
in extending the length of his heat and does not care to
slag out, he might in some cases use coal to advantage.
Some founders make the bed of coal and use coke only for
the charges, while others mix the coal and coke together all
the way through the heat. It generally takes a less weight
of coke than of coal to melt iron, but owing to coke being
lighter than coal, a given weight of it will stand higher
above the tuyeres or will be deeper between the charges.
For this reason, the charges of iron are generally made
heavier when using coal than coke; for, if the same weights
of coal and iron are used that work well with coke and iron,
there will not be sufficient coal in some cases to divide the
charges of iron properly.

74. Manufacture of Coke.—Coke is made by driving
the volatile matter out of certain kinds of bituminous coal.
This operation is called coking, and is carried on in special
kilns or in ovens. Coke differs from coal in structure, for
the driving out of the volatile matter leaves the coke more
porous than the coal from which it was made. Carbon and

ash are the two chief components of coke. The greater the amount of fixed carbon and the less ash the coke contains, the better are its melting qualities. Another component that may give trouble if it exceeds .85 per cent. is sulphur. This must be watched very carefully, as coke with much sulphur will harden the iron and do much harm when soft castings are desired. A coke possessing a silvery bright metallic luster and a solid body, with cells well connected and of a uniform structure, is generally a good fuel for melting iron.

TABLE V.

ANALYSES OF COKE.

Where Made.	Fixed Carbon.	Ash.	Sulphur.
Connellsville, Pa., average of 3 samples............	86.96	9.74	.810
Chattanooga, Tenn., average of 4 samples........	80.61	16.34	1.595
Birmingham, Ala., average of 4 samples............	87.29	10.54	1.195
Pocahontas, Va., average of 3 samples............	92.53	5.74	.597
New River, W. Va., average of 8 samples........	92.38	7.21	.562
Big Stone Gap, Ky., average of 7 samples........	93.23	5.69	.749

75. Analysis of Coke.—The kind of coke generally condemned by founders is small-sized coke mixed with coke-dust, or coke that is dark in general appearance and soft in quality. Even when coke has all the other desirable qualities but is small in size, it is liable to produce bad results in melting. A coke may not possess the desired silvery bright metallic luster, and may be of a dark color having black ends, and still be good, if it is only large and of a hard uniform character and possesses a good structure. In Table V is given the percentages of fixed carbon, ash, and sulphur in coke made in various sections of the United States.

***

ECONOMY OF FUEL IN MELTING IRON.

76. Ratio of Weights of Iron and Fuel.—Every now and then some one reports melting in the ratio of 1 to 10 or 12, and others dispute it, claiming that it is good practice to melt 5 to 7 pounds of iron with 1 pound of fuel. The man melting only in the ratio of 1 to 5 or 7 may be doing better work than the one melting in the ratio of 1 to 10 or 12. These ratios depend entirely on shop conditions, the character of the castings, fuel, and iron, and also the manner of managing the heats. For example, take two 40-inch cupolas, with the same height of tuyeres and with a capacity of 9 tons when not slagged. One shop may be called on to melt 4 to 5 tons in one of these cupolas, while another might be required to melt 30 tons, each having the same class of fuel and iron. There is little difference in the height of the bed, in the first place, for either of these extremes of tonnage, and to keep up the bed to its proper height, about the same weight of fuel will be required between the charges. Figuring up the ratio or percentage of fuel to iron each of these founders should use, it is found, taking 1,000 pounds for the bed and 200 pounds between the charges, that the one melting 4 tons of iron would use 1,600 pounds of fuel, a ratio of 1 to 5, while the one melting 30 tons of iron would use 5,800 pounds of fuel, a ratio of a little better than 1 to 10. This difference comes largely from the fact that if but 1 ton of iron were to be melted, it would require about as much fuel in the bed or above the top of the tuyeres as if 30 tons had to be melted. Furthermore, where the heats may be of the same weight, in the same sized cupolas and the same height of lower tuyeres, one man may have the best of fuel and clean medium-sized iron that is not required to be melted very hot for his work, while the other man may have conditions that are the reverse in every particular. When such a difference in conditions prevails, one might melt 4 tons with a ratio of 1 to 8, while the other could not do better than 1 to 4. It is not economy for any founder to cut down so closely on fuel as to get a dull iron when his work demands hot iron, and any one following this practice will find that the castings lost by dull iron and the expense of taking care of bunged ladles, cupolas, etc. will greatly exceed in cost that of the additional fuel that should have been used. On the other hand, there is no excuse for using large quantities of fuel, for often better melting can be done with less fuel.

MELTING IRON IN SMALL CUPOLAS.

77. Construction of Small Cupolas.— There are often cases where it is desired to melt iron on a small scale for commercial or experimental purposes. By reading the description of modern cupolas, many are led to think that these must be available in order to melt iron; this is not the case, however. Iron has actually been melted in an old flour barrel that was lined with clay and pieces of brick. Iron has been successfully melted in a 12-inch cupola having the blast furnished by a blacksmith's bellows. In this case the cupola was placed on a wagon and wheeled through the streets in an industrial exhibition of a large city's manufacturing establishments. It was not a special device, but one made from an old piece of a 16-inch sheet-iron pipe, 24 inches long, set on a flat plate, with $1\frac{1}{2}$-inch holes on each side of the pipe about 3 inches from the bottom for tuyere holes, to admit the blast from the bellows. This little improvised cupola was kept in blast for about 1 hour and melted 200 pounds of small pieces of iron.

78. Cupolas for Experimental Work.—In Fig. 11 is shown a cupola made of a piece of an old cupola shell, lined with 4-inch brick, that was placed alongside of a regular cupola and used for experimental purposes and for making small repair work when the large cupolas were not in blast. This cupola has melted 500 pounds of iron at one heat, and is illustrated here to show how readily and cheaply one can devise a cupola that will melt small quantities of iron.   The

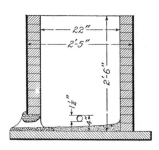

FIG. 11.

fuel and iron used for charging such cupolas must be small in size.   The cupola shown in Fig. 11 is 22 inches inside diameter and 30 inches outside diameter; its height is 32 inches, and the two tuyeres, having a diameter of $1\frac{1}{2}$ inches, are placed 4 inches above the bottom plate at opposite sides of the shell.

79. Chinese Cupola.—A Chinese cupola is shown in Fig. 12, which is made in three sections placed on each other.   The sections consist of riveted boiler-plate shells lined with fireclay, and have handles *a*, two on each side, for the purpose of lifting them apart by means of two bars. The upper section is open and enlarged at the top, and receives the charge of iron and fuel.   The blast is supplied to the middle section through a single tuyere and a pipe *b* that carries the blast from the blower *c*.   The blower is operated by hand and consists of a rectangular box *c* with the interior arranged in compartments, each of which is fitted with a plunger operated by means of a rod *d* and handle *e*. As the tap hole *f* of the cupola is at the floor

FIG. 12.

level it is necessary to place the receiving ladle in a pit in order to be under the spout *g*. The capacity of this cupola is about 80 Chinese plowshares per day.

AIR FURNACES.

GENERAL CONSTRUCTION OF AN AIR FURNACE.

80. Introduction.—One form of **reverberatory**, or **air, furnace** is shown in Fig. 13 (*a*) and (*b*), and receives the name because of its form and because the natural draft is generally used to operate it as distinguished from the blast or forced draft used in the cupola.

These furnaces are used for melting iron for heavy work when purity and great strength of metal are desired, such as for large bells, rolls, etc.   Massive scrap iron can be most easily melted in a reverberatory furnace, as the charging can be done by the aid of a crane.   The greatest strength of casting is obtained with a reverberatory furnace, because it

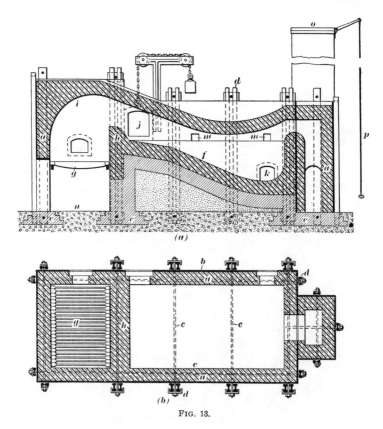

FIG. 13.

is possible to get a high percentage of combined carbon with a low percentage of sulphur.   The character of the mixture can be observed in an air furnace and tested, and the necessary changes, if any, made with comparative ease before tapping.   The metal is purer than that from the cupola, as it is not in contact with the fuel during the melting, and a charge can be melted without changing to any appreciable degree the percentage of carbon originally contained.

On the other hand, there is a considerable loss by oxidation and scintillation, which may amount to as much as 12 per cent., and much greater skill is required to operate such furnaces as compared with cupolas. If the charge should chill, it is generally necessary to tear down the furnace to remove the cold metal; and being so massive, the further expensive operation of blasting with dynamite has sometimes to be resorted to in order to break it into pieces that can be handled.

81. Form and Dimensions.—The body of an air furnace consists of a box of rectangular form made of firebrick, as shown in vertical section in Fig. 13 (*a*), and in horizontal section in (*b*). The walls *a* are made extra thick and tight, so as to retain the heat and prevent any leakage of cold air into the furnace. The brickwork is incased in cast-iron or wrought-iron plates *b*, and the whole is securely bound together with anchor rods *c* running both crosswise and lengthwise through the furnace, but in such locations as not to be affected by the heat, and buck stays *d* on the sides and ends of the furnace.

82. Foundation.—As the furnace is massive and not a self-contained steel vessel like the cupola, the foundation must receive special attention in its construction. Heavy stresses are produced by the great heat and by the weight of the charge, and the furnace is liable to crack or settle, resulting in the loss of the molten metal. The footings *e* of the furnace walls rest on a bed of concrete that extends under the whole furnace.

83. The Hearth.—The bottom covering, or **hearth,** *f*, is made of sand and clay, and is supported by substantial brickwork. When melting an extra heavy piece of metal, firebrick piers, extending above the sand bottom, are sometimes used to support it free from the sand so the flame can play entirely around the piece.

84. Minor Parts.—The grate g is 3 or 4 feet long
and the full width of the furnace. A bridge wall h from
10 to 15 inches high separates the grate from the hearth f.
The crown i of the furnace is vaulted so as to deflect the
flame on to the iron placed on the hearth, and the hearth,
crown, and bridge wall must be so arranged as to secure
the full effect of the heat where it is needed in melting. A
charging opening j of liberal proportions is located either on
the side or on the top of the furnace. It has a metal cover
lined with firebrick. If located on the side, the door usually
opens by sliding upwards and is operated by counterbalance
weights and chains over pulleys or by levers, as shown in
Fig. 13 (a). When the opening is on top, both the door
and the charge may be lifted by means of a crane. An
opening k is used for cleaning out the furnace and as
an entrance for making repairs. Fireclay, daubing, and
cementing are required in repairing the lining of air furnaces the same as is done in making repairs of cupola
linings. The spout is located at the lowest part of the hearth
and is made and attached the same as in a cupola. As it is
important to keep the surface of the metal clean, holes m
for skimming are located above the hearth. There is also
an opening for introducing a hand ladle for samples to be
tested. Peep holes are necessary to observe the melting
process. The ash-pit n is made low, so as to give plenty of
air space for the draft. Frequently the hearth of a reverberatory furnace is made more nearly level and the roof
nearly parallel to the hearth. At times the roof is made in
sections, so that it can be removed for charging. Such furnaces are illustrated and described in *Malleable Casting*.

85. The Chimney.—The **chimney** for an air furnace
is constructed of firebrick, rectangular in section, and about
equal in area to that of the air-space area of the grate. The
height ranges from 30 to 80 feet, or whatever is necessary to
secure a strong draft. It is fitted with a regulating damper o
on top that is operated from the ground by means of a rod p.
The chimney is preferably constructed on a separate

foundation from the body of the furnace, so as not to be injured by any movement of the furnace caused by the effects of the heat, and also to permit changes and repairs in the furnace.

86. Firing and Charging.—The furnace should be heated 5 or 6 hours before charging. The whole charge is then put in at once and all openings closed as tight as possible, permitting no air to enter except through the fire. The charge is stacked on the hearth in an open pile. If of pigs, the first layer is put lengthwise, with spaces between for the flame to enter; the next bars are laid crosswise, and so on until all the pigs are in. If the charge is a mixture of different sized pieces and kinds of iron, the smallest and easiest melted pieces are placed in the bottom, where they will receive the least heat.

As the charge is not placed in the fuel, as it is in the cupola, but in the flame, which has something of a blowpipe action, bituminous coal and gas are the fuels used, because they produce the most flame. Anthracite coal can be used by special draft arrangements, but it is objectionable on account of the ashes settling on the surface of the molten metal, necessitating skimming.

87. Boiling the Metal.—Boiling is a process which consists in inserting green-wood poles in the melted charge in an air furnace, causing a violent ebullition and a thorough mixing of the different grades of iron melted together. This process is also called **poling**. It is also necessary to stir the unmelted pieces in the basin, breaking them up with puddling bars.

OIL-BURNING FURNACES.

88. Construction of Oil-Burning Furnace.—In Fig. 14 is shown a furnace for melting metal by means of crude petroleum as fuel. The furnace consists of a cylinder a made of sheet steel, with cast-iron heads b, b, and lined with firebrick c. The door of the furnace consists of a circular hole d in the side of the shell. The shell is mounted on trunnions e, e and can be revolved by means of a capstan handle f at one end.

The oil burner is located in one of the trunnions, which is hollow, and consists of a $\frac{1}{8}$-inch oil tube g placed in a 3-inch air pipe h. The oil tube g is forked at the inner end, and the openings through which the oil passes in a spray consists

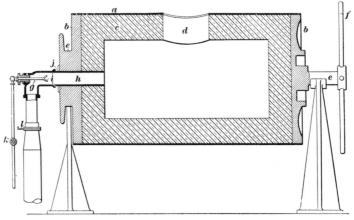

FIG. 14.

of a number of narrow slots in the flattened ends of the two prongs i of the tube. The axis of both these pipes is placed so as to coincide with that of the furnace a, and the air pipe h is connected to the shell by means of a sleeve joint j, so that the shell may be revolved without disturbing the burner. The oil pipe is fitted with a needle valve k for regulating the supply, and the air pipe has a gate valve l.

89. Operation of an Oil-Burning Furnace.—The operation of an oil-burning furnace is simple. The air blast under a pressure of from 8 to 10 ounces is first turned on, and a piece of flaming material, such as wood, paper, or waste, saturated with oil, introduced into the furnace. The oil at about 3 pounds pressure is then admitted. The first ignition causes a puff of heavy smoke due to the excess of oil in the material used to start the fire, but this immediately clears away and complete combustion ensues. The jet of flame is blown against the opposite head of the cylinder, whence it reverberates, filling the entire space with flame. The temperature is such as to make the firebrick lining white hot in about 25 minutes with a consumption of about 6 gallons of oil. When this temperature is reached, metal in the required quantity is introduced directly into the cylinder, which is revolved so that the opening d is brought to any convenient position for this purpose. The furnace is then revolved and the opening brought to the top, and a crucible, having the bottom removed, is set into the opening like a hopper. This hopper is filled with pieces of the metal to be melted. The flame is now lengthened by adjusting the oil and air valves until it escapes through the crucible and gradually melts the contained metal, which drops into the heavier part of the charge in the cylinder. The crucible also serves to protect the edges of the hole in the shell from the flame.

From 20 to 25 minutes are required to melt a charge of brass in this manner; 25 minutes for copper; about 1 hour for cast iron, and a slightly longer time for steel. The consumption of oil is at the rate of about 12 gallons per hour in a furnace of 1,200 pounds capacity. When the charge is melted, the furnace is revolved on its trunnions and the molten metal poured into the ladles.

MIXING CAST IRON.

MAKING CAST IRON.

THE BLAST FURNACE.

INTRODUCTION.

1. Occurrence of Iron in Nature.—Iron is the most widely distributed of any of the metals; yet it is never found chemically pure in nature, except perhaps in some meteorites, where it is a mere curiosity of no practical value. There are many iron minerals, but only a few of them constitute useful ores of iron on account of the fact that many contain either too low a percentage of iron or elements that render them unfit for the manufacture of *cast iron* or *steel*. **Iron ore** may be defined as any iron-bearing mineral from which the metal can be extracted at a profit. This definition will bar out many minerals containing a large percentage of iron on account of the impurities that they contain; and on the other hand, it will admit many that carry a low percentage of iron, but no injurious elements. The ores of iron are oxides and carbonates. Formerly the harder magnetic ores and the hard hematites and carbonates were preferred, but with modern blast-furnace practice, the softer and more easily reduced ores are coming into more general use. In the United States very few furnaces are running on ore containing less than 50 per cent. iron. The

§ 47

remainder of the ore is composed of oxygen, silicon, phosphorus, lime, sulphur, magnesia, aluminum, manganese, titanium, etc. Some ores also contain organic matter. Most of the impurities occur in very small amounts. The rich ores of iron contain from 60 to 68 per cent. metallic iron, while those low in iron, called lean ores, may contain only from 30 to 40 per cent.

2. Nature of Cast Iron. — Chemically pure iron is soft and ductile, and can be forged and welded, but its melting point is so high and its character is such that it cannot be used for making castings. The iron commonly known as **cast iron** contains some impurities that lower its fusing point and that change its characteristics materially. Wrought iron fuses above 3,000° F., while cast iron melts at about 2,200° F. Carbon is the element that makes the greatest change, though several other elements are active in producing changes; these with their effects will be taken up later. The fracture of cast iron varies from a coarse semicrystalline gray to a fine, close-grained, white fracture. Formerly all iron was graded by its appearance when broken; now it is generally graded according to its chemical composition.

CONSTRUCTION OF BLAST FURNACE.

3. Form and Dimensions of Blast Furnaces. The iron is reduced from its ores by fusing them with lime in a **blast furnace,** the lime being obtained by the use of limestone, marble, shells, etc. A blast furnace consists of a tall shaft into which alternate layers of fuel, flux, and iron ore are introduced. The blast furnace is continuous in its operation; all the material charged into the top of the furnace is reduced to a liquid condition and tapped out at the bottom. Blast furnaces are much larger than *cupolas,* the height of the furnace depending somewhat on the fuel and ore used. A furnace capable of handling from 175 to 200 tons of ore in 24 hours is about 70 feet high and 14 feet internal diameter at the largest part. Like a cupola furnace, a blast furnace is usually made of an iron shell lined with some refractory substance; but unlike most cupolas, the lower portion of the furnace that has to withstand the greatest heat is generally provided with water coolers built into the lining. These coolers usually consist of pipes arranged in sections, so that the water can be shut off from any one for repairs. Owing to the great weight of the furnace and its charge, very substantial foundations are necessary.

OPERATION OF BLAST FURNACE.

4. Fuels Used in a Blast Furnace.—The best and purest grades of cast iron are made in blast furnaces using charcoal for fuel. This is on account of the fact that the charcoal does not contain as much sulphur as coal or coke, and also because the ash is of such a nature that the impurities pass into the slag rather than into the iron. Owing to the soft, friable nature of charcoal, it will not sustain so great a burden as coke or coal; hence, it is impossible to use as high a blast furnace with this fuel as when coke or coal is used. Charcoal blast furnaces are rarely more than 30 or 40 feet in height, and are of comparatively small capacity. Charcoal iron is made only from the purest and richest ores and is used for special lines of manufacture. Coke and coal, especially anthracite coal, are the chief fuels used in blast furnaces. Owing to the strength of these fuels it is possible to carry a much higher burden in the furnace; hence, the furnaces using coal or coke for fuel range from 65 to 100 feet in height; they are also larger in diameter than those burning charcoal. All coke and coal contain more or less sulphur that will injure the iron to a greater or less extent, and these fuels also contain a large amount of ash that must be fluxed and removed with the slag.

According to the statistics of the American Iron and Steel Association, there were made in the United States during 1901, 13,782,386 tons of coke iron, 1,668,808 tons of anthracite and coke iron mixed, 43,719 tons of anthracite iron, 360,146 tons of charcoal iron, and 23,294 tons of charcoal and coke iron mixed.

5. Temperature of the Blast Used in a Blast Furnace.—Formerly all blast furnaces used cold blast, as in cupola practice, but it has been found that this greatly reduces the temperature of the furnace at or near the melting zone, and consequently decreases its capacity, so that now the blast is usually heated to a greater or less extent in blast-furnace work. At present the cold blast is used only in a few charcoal furnaces. A warm blast ranging from 250° to 400° F., or a hot blast ranging from 700° to 1,100° F., is more commonly used in the average furnace, while some furnaces use a superheated blast having a temperature of from 1,100° to 1,600° F. There are two general methods used for heating the blast. In one, the escaping gases from the furnace are allowed to pass around iron pipes through which the blast is drawn. In the other, the escaping gases from the furnace are allowed to burn in a chamber filled with *brick checkerwork*, this being composed of bricks loosely piled up, as in a brick kiln. After the bricks are sufficiently heated the gases are turned into another chamber; the blast for the furnace is heated by being drawn through the chamber containing the heated bricks. The temperature of the blast used in coke or anthracite iron furnaces usually ranges from 1,000° to 1,300° F. The pressure of the blast in standard furnaces varies from 5 to 25 pounds per square inch, and the weight of the blast used in making iron is greater than that of all the fuel, iron, and limestone combined. The air for the blast is compressed to the desired pressure by blowing engines.

6. Charging a Blast Furnace.—The charge of iron, coke, and limestone is made up of the proper proportions of each by weight and hoisted to the platform at the top of the furnace and dumped into the hopper, which is closed at the bottom by a conical casting called the *bell*. After the proper

amount of charge has been distributed around the bell, it is
lowered and the charge allowed to fall into the furnace,
after which the bell is raised to its proper position, closing
the top of the furnace and making it gas-tight.

7. Reactions in a Blast Furnace. — The blast is
regulated so as not to burn completely the carbon of the
fuel. Some of the carbon is burned to carbonic oxide, which
is a gas composed of 1 atom of carbon and 1 atom of oxygen,
or CO, and some of it to carbon dioxide, which is a gas composed of 1 atom of carbon and 2 atoms of oxygen, or CO_2.
The hot carbonic oxide passing through the charge reacts
on the ore, taking oxygen from it, and becomes the gas
called carbon dioxide. This extraction of oxygen from the
ore reduces the iron oxide to metallic iron, and this in turn
takes up more or less carbon and settles to the melting zone,
which is from 2 to 4 feet above the tuyeres. At this point
all the constituents of the charge are rendered fluid. From
10 to 30 per cent. of the ore and from 10 to 14 per cent. of
the fuel charged into a blast furnace are composed of
earthy matter and ash, which must be carried off as slag. A
portion of this earthy matter is basic, and the remainder is
acid. If the basic and the acid portions are equal, the ore
will be self-fluxing and form a slag without the addition of
any other material; but in most cases some acid element,
such as silicon, predominates, and this necessitates the
addition of limestone as a flux to carry off the excess of
silicon. If either too much lime or too much silicon is
present, the slag will be thick; if approximately the right
amount of each is present, the slag will be very thin and
fluid, so that it will separate thoroughly from the iron. As
the charge descends in the furnace, the limestone is converted to quicklime by the heat that drives off the carbon
dioxide. The moisture in the charge is also driven out by
the heat. Owing to the fact that the slag is lighter than
the iron, it floats on the surface of the latter and is tapped
off through a separate and higher tap hole just previous to
tapping for iron.

The proportions of fuel, limestone, and ore must be carefully calculated; for if the ore is not properly reduced, a portion of the iron will pass into the slag. In this case the iron obtained will be low in silicon and high in sulphur. This may also be due to an insufficient amount of heat, on account of which much partly reduced iron arrives at the melting point and the silicon is all utilized in carrying off the unreduced iron ore. When a furnace is working in this manner, it is said to be *working cold*. A larger percentage of fuel and an increase in the heat of the blast make the furnace *work hot* and cause the iron to absorb more silicon.

8. The carbon in pig iron is obtained from the fuel of the furnace, and the total amount of carbon that iron will absorb depends on the working conditions of the furnace and on the percentages of silicon, manganese, and sulphur in the iron. This characteristic of manganese is shown in the manufacture of spiegeleisen, which is rich in manganese, and for this reason may contain as much as 6 per cent. of carbon. In case the iron contains less than .75 per cent. of manganese, it cannot carry much, if any, more than 3.5 per cent. of carbon, though in rare cases it may contain over 4 per cent. It is claimed that if chromium is substituted for manganese, it will enable iron to absorb as much as 12 per cent. of carbon.

9. The sulphur in iron is obtained chiefly from the fuel, only a small portion of it coming from the ore and the fluxes. If limestone is used as a flux, and the slag is hot and fluid, it will usually absorb and carry off a large amount of the sulphur; while if the slag is allowed to get thick and sluggish, and the furnace is working cold, more of the sulphur will go into the iron. Low-sulphur or high-grade pig iron is generally obtained by having a hot furnace well, but not excessively, fluxed with lime. High-silicon iron and iron that is also high in sulphur may be obtained by having a hot furnace poorly fluxed with lime. When the furnace is working hot with a thin slag, the silicon tends to go into the iron and the sulphur into the slag.

10. Tapping a Blast Furnace.—Owing to the fact that the slag is lighter than iron, it floats on the surface of the latter; it is tapped from a hole at the side of the furnace and is generally run into suitable cars and removed from the furnace, while the iron is tapped from a hole at the front of the furnace, and is either run directly into the pig bed or into a ladle, from which it is taken to a pig bed or a casting machine; or it may be taken to a converter or an open-hearth furnace and be made directly into steel without remelting.

CASTING PIG IRON.

11. Using Sand Molds for Casting Pig Iron. The metal as it flows from a blast furnace is run either into sand or iron molds. If the former are used, the iron flows from the tap hole down a long runner having an incline of about 1 foot in 18 feet. From this it is led by branch runners on each side to the pig-bed molds. Each of these branch runners, as it fills up, is stopped off with an iron cutter driven into the main runner a few feet above the branch opening; another branch runner is then opened by pulling away the sand that divides the main runner from it. This operation is continued until the uppermost pig bed, which is nearest the furnace, is filled, at which time the furnace is generally freed of its metal for that tap. When the pigs have become solid enough not to bleed, that is, let molten iron flow out when broken, sand to a depth of about $\frac{1}{4}$ inch is thrown over them. One or two gangs of men wearing shoes having heavy wooden soles now start at the lower end to break the pigs away from the sows, or branch runners, by means of long pointed bars. After the pigs are separated, the sows are broken into small pieces by the use of bars and sledges.

A bed of 500 pigs and 18 sows can be broken in about 30 minutes by 3 men. After being broken, a large stream of water is turned on to cool the metal, so that it can be loaded on cars or piled in the storage yard. The floor of the casting house is usually divided into two or more sections, so that the different operations can be carried on continuously.

12. Using Iron Molds for Casting Pig Iron.—In order to avoid the heavy sand scale that forms on pigs cast in sand molds, and also to avoid the labor of making up the pig bed, pig iron is cast in iron molds. In some cases the iron molds are placed in the pig bed itself. These molds are from 6 to 10 feet long and usually somewhat greater in cross-section than for the ordinary pig. Before the iron is allowed to flow into the molds, they are sprinkled with a wash of clay or lime water; the water evaporates and leaves a coating that prevents the iron sticking to the surface of the molds. The iron is conducted to the molds by means of the ordinary runners and branches. Owing to the great weight of these pigs, they have to be handled and broken by mechanical means. More or less trouble has been experienced in the cracking and breaking of the large molds, and occasionally from the difficulty of removing the iron from them, although, owing to the great length of the pigs, the contraction usually frees them without any difficulty.

13. Pig Casting Machines. — In order to make the casting process continuous, various forms of casting machines have been invented. Practically all of them produce small pigs that do not require much, if any, breaking before being charged into the cupola. There are two general styles of casting machines; in one style a series of molds moves around on an endless link belt or chain. The molds are given a coating of lime water as they run along the under side of the conveyer, the lime water being splashed into the molds by a suitable mechanism. Just after the molds come from the wheel at the head end of the conveyer, they receive the molten metal from the ladle. The pigs cool as they are carried down the conveyer, and the contraction, together with the coating of lime on the molds, frees them from the molds. At the lower end of the conveyer there is usually arranged an automatic knocking device to insure the removal of the pigs from the molds. These casting machines are frequently arranged to load the pigs directly into cars.

In the other style of casting machines, the short molds are arranged radially around the periphery of a large wheel, and the iron is poured into the molds at one point and dumped out at the opposite side as the wheel slowly rotates on a vertical axis; the molds are coated with a suitable wash as they return to the ladle. In the operation of casting machines the iron is taken to them in ladles and frequently one machine or group of machines receive the iron from several furnaces. The fact that the metal is caught in a ladle before being poured into the molds gives a much more uniform product than is possible by the old method of casting pigs in beds. Also the iron being free from sand scale, there will be less dirt in the cupola and less fuel will be required for remelting the iron.

14. Segregation in Pig Iron.—Very frequently pigs taken from different parts of the same cast are found to vary greatly in composition. It is not uncommon for the metal to contain 1 per cent. more of silicon at one end of a tap than at the other, and to have a difference of over .05 per cent. in sulphur. The results from the analyses of the pigs from 6 beds are shown in Table I. The beds are numbered as they were cast, No. 1, being the farthest from the furnace, received the iron first, and No. 6 last. Table II shows the results from the same furnace under normal conditions. These tables show what unsatisfactory results a founder may expect when using furnace casts of iron that are so irregular in their silicon and sulphur contents. They also show the wisdom of thoroughly mixing furnace casts of iron before they are charged into a cupola, when uniform results are desired in castings.

TABLE I.

ANALYSES OF PIG BEDS IN A CHANGEABLE FURNACE.

Number of Bed.	1	2	3	4	5	6
Per Cent. Silicon	.600	.680	.700	1.00	1.250	2.200
Per Cent. Sulphur	.084	.071	.062	.05	.042	.027

TABLE II.

ANALYSES OF PIG BEDS WITH FURNACE IN NORMAL CONDITION.

Number of Bed.	1	2	3	4	5	6
Per Cent. Silicon	2.180	2.180	2.22	2.230	2.250	2.250
Per Cent. Sulphur	.021	0.021	.02	.019	.019	.019

Some furnacemen make an effort to mix their pig iron thoroughly, so as to give uniform results even from irregular casts of iron. This will be appreciated, as few founders have any opportunity for mixing the iron before being charged into the cupola. Silicon and sulphur are the elements most unevenly distributed in furnace casts of pig iron, as phosphorus and manganese rarely, if ever, vary sufficiently to change the grade of a brand of iron, at least not to such an extent as is done by silicon and sulphur.

15. Grading Pig Iron.—Previous to 1892 most furnacemen had their pig iron graded entirely by the appearance of the fracture. The iron having the most open grain was called No. 1, the next in order No. 2, and so on up to Nos. 5 or 7. The high numbers generally indicated a mottled or white grade of iron, giving hard iron in castings. Since furnacemen commenced to make iron by analyzing the ores, fluxes, and fuels that go into the furnace, and the iron and slag that come out of it, they have learned that the appearance of the fracture of iron is generally deceptive and that the only safe guide to depend on is the analysis of the iron in defining its grade. This is due to the fact that the size and character of the grain in pig iron depend largely on the rate of cooling.

If two castings be made from the same pattern, poured from the same ladle and gates, one being formed in sand and the other in iron, so as to make a difference in the rate of cooling, it will be found that the one cast in the iron mold, and hence cooled first, will be much closer in grain than the one cast in sand, and cooled more slowly. The rate of cooling always affects the grain of cast iron. When it is considered that there are rarely two casts of pig iron that come out of the furnace alike in fluidity, that fill the pig molds in the same length of time, or that give the same size of pigs, it is evident that the grain of the iron, as exposed by fracture, will vary greatly. There are still some of the old-school founders who think that they can judge pig iron by fracture, and when they do not get the results from the cupola mixtures that they expected, they will excuse the bad work on the ground that the fuel was bad, or that there was a mistake in charging by getting the wrong iron, or that they had poor blast, or that the wind was blowing the wrong way, etc.

Many interesting experiments have been made to determine the relation between the grain of pig iron and its chemical composition, and it has been found that the grain does not depend on the chemical composition so much as on the rate of cooling, and that pig iron should be graded according to its analysis and not according to its grain.

16. For melting two different kinds of cast iron under exactly similar conditions, a twin cupola, as shown in Fig. 1, may be used. This is simply a small cupola having a tap hole *a* on each side and a brick dividing wall *b* in the center.

At the lower part of the furnace there is an arch c connecting the two sides, but the sand bed d is made high in the middle and the charging is done in such a manner that there is practically no chance for the iron charged on each side of the partition b to mix.

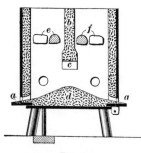

FIG. 1.

In an experiment with the double cupola shown in Fig. 1, two pieces of pig iron were melted in it. One of these possessed a very open grain, which, judging from the fracture, would make the softest kind of casting. Analysis, however, showed that it would produce a hard casting. The other pig was close grained and the surface full of blowholes, such as usually occur in the presence of a large amount of sulphur, so that judging from its fracture it would produce a hard casting, though the analysis showed that a soft casting would be produced from it. The first contained 1.25 per cent. of silicon and .035 per cent. of sulphur, while the second had 2.86 per cent. of silicon and .04 per cent. of sulphur. The iron obtained by melting both pigs was cast in exactly similar molds, each mold being provided with one gate and arranged to produce a number of castings of various thicknesses, the end of all the castings being against a chill, so as to determine the chilling effect. The iron from the first specimen, which had appeared soft in the pig, gave very hard castings that in the case of the thinner castings could not be machined at all, while that from the second pig, which had appeared hard, gave very soft castings that could easily be machined. In the first casting, which appeared soft, the chilling of the ends of the specimens was marked, while the castings from the second pig, which appeared hard, showed practically no chilling whatever.

CALCULATING CAST-IRON MIXTURES.

COMPOSITION OF CAST IRON.

ELEMENTS CONTAINED IN PIG IRON.

17. Composition of Pig Iron.—The **pig iron** made by blast furnaces generally contains from 92 to 96 per cent. of metallic iron. The other 4 to 8 per cent. consists chiefly of impurities in the form of sulphur, phosphorus, carbon, manganese, and silicon. While it is true that the five elements mentioned are impurities in iron, they are really the elements that make cast iron of commercial value, as pure iron is worthless for making castings. The physical qualities required in pig iron for the construction of castings depend almost entirely on the percentages of the above elements present.

18. Elements That Are Fairly Constant in Pig Iron.—All the best blast furnaces are provided with pyrometers for measuring the temperature of the escaping gases and of the blast. This enables the manager to control the heat in the furnace very closely and thus, in a large measure, prevent irregularities arising from this source. The temperature and pressure of the blast are important factors affecting the regularity of furnace operation.

Ordinarily the phosphorus in the iron will remain fairly constant as long as the same fuels, ores, and fluxes are used, even though the furnace may be working quite irregularly.

Manganese can also be kept practically constant if the heat of the furnace can be closely controlled, and even when a furnace works quite irregularly, the percentage of manganese will not vary greatly with the same ores, fuel, and fluxes.

19. Elements That Vary in Pig Iron.—Even with the greatest care in the control of a blast furnace, it is impossible to keep the percentage of certain of the elements in pig iron constant. Those having the greatest variation are silicon, sulphur, and carbon. The percentage of silicon depends very largely on whether the furnace is working hot or cold. A hot furnace with plenty of fuel will tend to put silicon into the iron, especially if it is well fluxed; if these conditions can be maintained, the percentage of silicon can be held fairly constant. But there are many irregularities that occur even with the greatest care in regulating the blast. The most common of these is called *scaffolding.* When this occurs, the charge becomes hung up in the furnace and then finally drops or slips down into the bosh, or into the crucible, thus suddenly bringing a large amount of comparatively cold material into the melting zone. When these conditions prevail, it is impossible to keep the silicon anywhere near constant.

The same cause that carries the silicon into the slag, i. e., low temperature, will reduce the power of the slag to carry off sulphur, and hence drives the sulphur into the iron.

The total percentage of carbon is not affected so much by the irregularities in the furnace, as by the fact that the higher the percentage of silicon, the less the power of the iron to absorb carbon; and as manganese remains fairly constant in any given furnace under stated conditions, the total percentage of carbon will generally decrease with an increase in the percentage of silicon.

KINDS OF PIG IRON.

20. Pig iron is now generally bought according to chemical analysis and not by fracture as formerly. Hence, the iron is graded with reference to the percentages of the metalloids contained. *Metalloids* are those non-metallic elements that resemble metal in some of their properties. The term is applied in founding to the several elements previously mentioned as impurities in the iron. There is an endless variety in the kinds of pig iron, but the following are the ones of most general use.

21. Bessemer iron is made with coke and anthracite fuels, and is used in the manufacture of steel ingots and their products, also ingot-mold castings. Regular Bessemer iron must not exceed .1 per cent. of phosphorus, 2.5 per cent. of silicon, and .05 per cent. of sulphur. The manganese can vary from .3 per cent. to 1 per cent. or over, according to the conditions required. Bessemer iron will not be accepted by steelmakers if over .1 per cent. in phosphorus, unless it is intended for making steel by the basic process, which is a method by which the greater part of the phosphorus can be removed from iron. If it goes over this limit, or is higher than .05 per cent. in sulphur, it is called "off Bessemer." Bessemer pig iron can be used only for castings that do not require much life or fluidity in the iron while liquid, as Bessemer iron, on account of its low phosphorus, loses its life or fluidity much quicker than iron possessing more phosphorus. As a rule, the combined carbon in Bessemer iron varies from .3 to 1.3 per cent., and the graphitic carbon from 3.45 to 1.8 per cent.

22. Foundry Iron. — There are several grades of **foundry iron.** They differ from Bessemer chiefly in the phosphorus, which may run up to 1 per cent. or over, and the silicon from 1 to 4 per cent. Sulphur must not exceed .05 per cent. The fracture of foundry iron cannot be told from that of Bessemer; neither is there much difference in their strength. Foundry iron flows better than Bessemer iron, and can be used for making more intricate castings.

23. Charcoal Iron. — As a rule, **charcoal iron** is stronger than either foundry or Bessemer iron, and differs from coke iron mainly in the carbon contents. It rarely contains more than 2 per cent. of silicon, and in most cases possesses less sulphur than is possible with any other brand of iron, while phosphorus and manganese occur about as in foundry iron and are quite constant. Usually charcoal iron can be distinguished from foundry or Bessemer iron by **its**

fracture, which is generally of a rich, dark, close, even texture. It is especially adapted to chill work, and by regulating the amount of silicon and carbon, it is possible to get any desired chill. Charcoal iron usually comes in smaller pigs than foundry or Bessemer iron. Its lower percentage of sulphur is due to its being made with charcoal fuel, which is practically free from sulphur; whereas coke or coal may contain 1 per cent. or more of sulphur, a great deal of which passes into the iron in the blast furnace. The total carbon will run from 2.5 to over 4.5 per cent.

24. Ferrosilicon contains from 6 to 16 per cent. of silicon, .01 up to .05 per cent. and over of sulphur, .5 to 1.5 per cent. of phosphorus, and often a high percentage of manganese, .2 to 3 per cent. or over, with the total carbon much lower than in foundry irons, .5 to 3 per cent., which is due to the fact that silicon reduces the power of iron to absorb carbon. The great variation that frequently occurs in the sulphur, phosphorus, and manganese should be watched carefully or else much injury may result from the use of ferrosilicon in foundry mixtures. This iron presents a silvery-white flaky fracture and possesses little strength. It is used chiefly in mixture with hard grades of pig iron or scrap to soften them. The high percentage of silicon in this iron is obtained by the use of highly silicious ores and an excess of fuel in the blast furnace. Ferrosilicon generally costs from $4 to $6 a ton more than foundry or Bessemer irons, the additional cost being largely due to the extra fuel required in its manufacture. In order to increase the silicon in foundry or Bessemer iron, the fuel in the blast furnace must be increased, thus adding to the cost of any iron high in silicon.

25. Gray forge iron is the cheapest iron made and rarely exceeds 1 per cent. of silicon. It is generally very high in sulphur, often exceeding .1 per cent. It may also be high in phosphorus and manganese. It is often derived from low grades of foundry iron and is chiefly used in the manufacture of water pipe, etc., and as mill iron in puddling furnaces to produce wrought iron.

26. Basic iron contains less than 1 per cent. of silicon and not over .05 per cent. of sulphur. The phosphorus may vary from .3 up to over 1 per cent., but rarely exceeds .4 per cent. The manganese is usually less than 1 per cent. It is used mostly in the manufacture of open-hearth steel.

EFFECT OF IMPURITIES ON PIG IRON.

27. Rare Elements in Pig Iron.—The physical properties of different brands of iron frequently show marked differences even when the chemical composition seems to be the same, as far as the elements ordinarily determined are considered. At times these differences cannot be accounted for by variations in the rate of cooling or other similar causes. It is probable that many of them are due to the presence of other elements than silicon, sulphur, phosphorus, manganese, or carbon. Among the other elements that are known to exist in some brands of pig iron are titanium, copper, nickel, sodium, magnesia, cobalt, chromium, aluminum, and tungsten. While these elements are not present in appreciable quantities in much of the iron of commerce, it is nevertheless probably true that many irregularities in the working of iron would be cleared up if determinations were made for these and possibly other elements. Titanium was formerly comparatively common in certain brands of iron, but on account of the difficulties that it gave, ores carrying much titanium are now very generally avoided. It is probable that during the next few years much will be learned as to the effect of these elements, and the foundry manager will then be able to control his mixtures better than at present.

28. Problems in Casting.—In the production of any desired class of castings there are two problems to be solved. The first is the production of an iron having the proper physical characteristics, and the second, the production of

the iron at the lowest possible cost.   To solve both of these
problems it is usually necessary to mix different grades of
pig iron and scrap together to obtain economical and practical mixtures.   When the great number of classes of castings that must be produced is considered, some idea can be
obtained as to the difficulty of adjusting all mixtures.   Among
the various classes may be mentioned chilled and sand rolls,
car wheels, ore and rock crushers, brake shoes, dies for
molding melted glass, cannon, shot and shell, engine and
machinery castings, electrical-machinery castings, hydraulic-
cylinder castings, ingot molds, annealing pots and kettles,
flywheels, stove-plate castings, lock hardware, sash weights,
etc.   Among these will be found all kinds of difficult requirements.   In the case of some of these castings considerable
variation in the grade of iron will not seriously affect them,
but in other cases a very small variation from the standard
required will make them totally worthless.

29.   Necessity for Chemical Analysis of Pig Iron.
The only way that some classes of castings can be produced
is by analyzing all the materials and carefully making the
proportions of the charges that go into the cupola.   It will
not do in all cases to depend on the analyses furnished by
the maker, as they usually have to be recorded several times
and pass through several hands, so that there is considerable
liability of making mistakes, and a very small mistake in some
of the elements will ruin some kinds of castings.   Then,
too, the analyses furnished may not give a fair average of
the shipment owing to the fact that the different elements
may segregate in different parts while casting pig iron.   In
order to insure a correct analysis, the founder should have
determinations made of samples of the iron as received.   As
a rule, most founders can control their iron sufficiently close
by having determinations made of the sulphur and silicon,
as the phosphorus, manganese, and total carbon will generally run fairly uniform in a given brand of iron from any
given furnace, and hence determinations for the last three
elements will not have to be made for every lot of metal.

30. Taking Samples for Chemical Analysis of Pig Iron.—The sampling of a given lot of iron is often a difficult problem. For ordinary purposes it is usually accurate enough to take one pig from near each end of the car and three or four others from different parts of the car, some from near the bottom and some from near the top, the whole number being about equally distributed throughout the load. These pigs should be broken in two and drillings taken from the center, care being taken that no sand from the outside of the pig becomes mixed with the drillings. There are different methods of drilling. A single hole in the center of each face is the most common practice. Other methods, especially for carbon determinations, require from 3 to 10 holes so distributed as to get the average composition of the pig. The use of a flat drill is recommended, as it gives the least variation in the size of the borings. The more important the work in hand, the greater should be the care taken in procuring samples. The drillings from the various pigs in any one lot should be thoroughly mixed and sealed in an envelope and delivered to the chemist, the envelope being carefully marked with the number of the car and such other information as will serve to designate the particular lot of iron in question. It requires about a half teaspoonful of the drillings for the determination of each element; if it is required to make determinations for silicon and sulphur, one teaspoonful might be sufficient, but in most cases it is best to send from three to four times this amount, so that the chemist can repeat his work if necessary.

In case of dispute, one method of sampling prescribes ten pigs, the buyer and seller each to select five. These are broken and drillings taken from the faces of the fractures. Drillings from the ten pigs, after being well mixed, are divided into three samples, one to be analyzed by the furnace, one by the foundry, and one by a disinterested chemist mutually agreed on. The average of the two analyses nearest alike is accepted as the chemical composition of the iron.

31. Standardized Drillings.—Sometimes two chemists cannot obtain like results on the same sample of iron. This may be due to differences in the method for making the analysis, or to some impurity in the chemicals used. In case of such disputes a check can usually be made by using standardized drillings, such as those furnished by the American Foundrymen's Association.

32. Carbon.—Iron has a strong affinity for **carbon,** and always contains an amount ranging from a few hundredths of 1 per cent. to possibly 12 per cent., depending on the amount of the other metalloids present, temperature, etc. Iron may absorb carbon without being fluid, as in the case-hardening process; similarly, it may give up a large portion without being entirely fluid, as in the making of malleable cast iron. As pig iron gets its carbon by absorption in the blast furnace, a high percentage of carbon is obtained by raising the temperature and increasing the fuel in the blast furnace. When pig iron is remelted in the cupola, it may either gain or lose carbon, depending on the original composition and the conditions in melting. While passing down the cupola, part of its carbon is burned out. The molten iron then comes in contact with the incandescent coke and absorbs more carbon. The hotter the iron and the longer its contact with the fuel, the more carbon it will absorb. But if the blast is heavy and the charge of the fuel small, more carbon may be oxidized than is gained so that the net result in the iron is a loss. The following experiment was made with low-silicon irons in a cupola supplied with plenty of fuel and operated hot: In an iron containing .82 per cent. silicon and .78 per cent. manganese, the total carbon was raised from 3.94 to 4.75 per cent. by remelting five times; and in steel scrap containing .31 per cent. silicon and .34 per cent. manganese, the total carbon was raised from .6 to 3.5 per cent. by remelting three times.

33. Carbon exists in iron in two distinct forms: *combined carbon,* forming the chemical compound carbide of iron; and *uncombined,* or *graphitic, carbon,* which is a

mechanical mixture with the iron. The physical properties
of iron depend largely on the state of the carbon. The iron
is soft or hard according to whether the carbon is free or
combined, and this ratio can be modified in two ways: by
varying the percentages of silicon, manganese, sulphur, and
phosphorus in the iron, and by varying the rate of cooling
and solidification. The thickness of the casting also influences the state of the carbon. When iron is liquid and hot,
the carbon is probably chemically combined, but as it cools
and solidifies some of the combined carbon changes to free
or graphitic carbon. An excess of free carbon can sometimes be seen on top of the cooling metal and is known as
kish, which in some cases rises in a cloud of black flakes from
the ladle; the addition of manganese or low-carbon iron, or
both, will prevent kish. Free carbon remains in the iron as
flakes of graphite, more or less filling the spaces between the
crystals. Manganese aids, and silicon hinders, the absorption of carbon. With much manganese present, the iron
may contain as high as 6 per cent. of carbon. But with
manganese under 1 per cent., the iron seldom contains more
than 4.5 per cent., the general average being about 3.5 per
cent. There is a wide range in the proportions of combined
and free carbon that make up the total carbon. This may
be effected either by the rate of cooling or by the other
elements contained in the iron. A cast iron with a total
carbon of 3.5 per cent. may by slow cooling be made to contain 3 per cent. of free or graphitic and .5 per cent. of combined carbon; while if chilled, these proportions may be
reversed.

If two castings of equal width and length be made, one
1 inch and the other 4 inches thick, and poured from the
same ladle at the same time, being left in the molds to cool
naturally and completely, the thin one will have a close,
dense grain, while the thick one will have a porous, open
grain, due wholly to the rate in cooling. The thin casting will have a much greater percentage of combined carbon than the thick one, as indicated by the difference in
grain.

34. A similar difference in structure can be produced by changes in silicon and sulphur. To make the 4-inch casting as dense as the 1-inch, use a mixture of iron having less silicon and more sulphur in the thick casting, allowing both castings the same length of time to cool, when the grain will be alike notwithstanding the difference in thickness. If liquid iron is poured into water or against an iron chill, the carbon will be less likely to take the graphitic form and the iron may have a hard, white, chilled body; whereas, were the same iron poured into a medium-thick casting and allowed to cool slowly, the iron would be gray and soft. The greater the percentage of total carbon, the more radically can the rate of cooling and the influence of the other elements affect it in taking a combined or graphitic form.

35. The combined carbon closes the grain of the iron, increases shrinkage, and increases the strength. Graphitic carbon weakens the iron and reduces shrinkage and chill, and makes a soft iron that is easily machined; but a smooth finish cannot be made if the percentage is very high.

36. Silicon.—On account of the fact that cast iron generally contains a larger percentage of **silicon** than any other of the elements, it is the safest and most convenient one to adopt as a base in regulating mixtures. Sulphur can neutralize from 10 to 15 parts of silicon, so that, if used as a base, the least error in its percentages will cause much more injury to the iron than slight errors made in silicon. The oxide of silicon is silica or pure sand. In passing through a cupola, iron always loses silicon, the amount depending on the quantity of blast and the percentage of silicon present. An increased blast brings more oxygen in contact with the iron in melting, and hence converts the silicon to silica. The higher the percentage of silicon, the greater the loss of silicon in the cupola. An iron running 4 per cent. in silicon may lose as much as 20 per cent. of the original amount, while the loss in very low silicon iron may not be perceptible. As the percentage of silicon in iron decreases, the difficulty of oxidizing it increases.

37. It has been stated that low-carbon pig gained in carbon under certain conditions when melted in a cupola. If iron is low in carbon and low in silicon, it will gain in carbon when remelted. Pure iron will absorb 6.67 per cent. of carbon, or 23 per cent. of silicon; hence, a given amount of carbon will produce 3½ times as much change on cast iron as the same amount of silicon. The percentage of silicon in cast iron varies with the amount of carbon it contains, and vice versa; the maximum amounts of each being impossible in any given iron at the same time. This ratio appears to exist in a remarkable degree. For every rise of .1 per cent. in carbon in pig iron made under the same conditions, there is a corresponding decrease of .35 per cent. in silicon, and vice versa. The same applies to cupola practice. When melting a pig of 3 per cent. carbon and 1 per cent. silicon, there may be a gain in carbon. With a small percentage of fuel, a high blast pressure, and a large percentage of carbon and silicon, there is a tendency toward a loss of carbon; while with a low blast pressure, a small percentage of carbon and silicon, and a large percentage of fuel, there is a tendency toward a gain in carbon during melting. Very high percentages of silicon decrease the fusibility of the iron.

38. Shrinkage depends more on the influence of silicon than any other metalloid. Every .2 per cent. increase of silicon decreases shrinkage about .01 inch per foot. Silicon not only reduces shrinkage but softens the iron by changing combined carbon into graphitic carbon, and also increases the length of time iron will remain in a molten state. As a rule, if more than 3 per cent. of silicon is contained in castings over ⅜ inch thick, with sulphur not over .06 per cent., it will cause castings to be soft and rotten or brittle. Silicon can be used to overcome many difficulties in casting and to control the quality and cheapness of mixtures containing scrap iron, but it must be used with care.

39. Sulphur.—Under ordinary conditions, iron melted in a cupola takes up **sulphur** from the fuel. The greater the amount of manganese in the iron, the less sulphur will be absorbed; and it is possible in cases of very high manganese iron to reduce the percentage of sulphur during melting, it passing off as a manganese sulphide in the slag. The ratio between the total amount of sulphur in the fuel and the amount absorbed by the iron depends on three conditions: (1) the kind and quality of flux used; (2) the temperature of the iron; (3) the composition of the coke and iron. The proper quantity of flux in a hot-working cupola will take care of a considerable amount of sulphur. The sulphur present in the fuel as a sulphureted hydrocarbon has no appreciable effect in increasing the percentage of sulphur in melted iron. This accounts for the fact that many foundries melting with coal obtain castings with a lower percentage of sulphur in proportion to the amount of sulphur in the fuel than do foundries melting with coke. An increase in sulphur, with the other elements and rate of cooling remaining constant, will harden iron by increasing the combined carbon and will also cause greater shrinkage, contraction, and chill. Sulphur shortens the time that iron can be kept fluid in a ladle; when it commences to show loss of fluidity, it cools off rapidly, making the iron run sluggishly and so bung up the ladle. It requires less change in the amount of sulphur to alter the softness or hardness of iron than any other element.

40. Where the fuel does not contain over .8 per cent. of sulphur, and the iron about .5 per cent. of manganese, the sulphur will increase in ordinary gray iron about .025 per cent. in one melting; but where coke contains 1 per cent. or over of sulphur, it may add to the iron from .04 per cent. to .08 per cent. of sulphur. This means that sometimes a casting will show .06 per cent. to .08 per cent. in sulphur when made from an iron having .02 per cent. of sulphur before remelting. This demonstrates the evils of high-sulphur fuel and the wisdom of analyzing both the fuels and the iron. An increase of .04 per cent. to .08 per cent. in sulphur in a casting can make intended soft castings so hard that they cannot be chipped or filed, this being especially true in the case of light work. One part of sulphur can neutralize the effect of 10 to 15 parts of silicon, the other elements and conditions remaining constant. Sulphur can be absorbed up to .3 per cent. in iron, increasing its fusibility, but decreasing the length of time that it will remain fluid. The presence of .2 per cent. of sulphur in any ordinary foundry mixture is sufficient to injure almost any class of castings, excepting sash weights, etc.

41. When a large percentage of sulphur is present in iron, it is very difficult to produce sound castings. The molten iron is usually sluggish and congeals quickly, thus enclosing escaping gases, dross, kish, etc., thereby producing blowholes and dirty castings. Such iron must be poured extra hot. The amount of sulphur in pig iron ranges from .01 per cent. to .08 per cent., and sometimes higher, but what is called a No. 1 iron, by analysis, generally contains from .01 per cent. to .03 per cent. of sulphur. No. 2 iron may have its sulphur run up to .06 per cent., but when it exceeds .08 per cent. it is usually classed as Nos. 4 to 6, which are often called mottled or white irons. Charcoal irons can be made more free from sulphur than any other class.

42. Manganese is a metal obtained from the ores. It has a white color, oxidizes readily, has a specific gravity of 8.01 (that of iron being 7.8), and requires from 200° to 500° higher temperature to melt than iron. Foundry, Bessemer, and charcoal irons contain from 2 per cent. to 3 per cent., and ferromanganese from 20 to 82 per cent. The general run of ordinary foundry pig irons contains from .5 per cent. to 2 per cent. of manganese. Manganese is not united with the iron as a chemical compound; it is rather alloyed with it, having practically no affinity for the iron.

Increasing manganese over .75 per cent., with the other elements remaining constant, creates greater contraction and chill on account of the fact that it hardens the iron. These effects of manganese may be very pronounced in light castings. A peculiarity of manganese is found in the fact that it may allow pig iron or castings to be open-grained and have the appearance of softness even when they are quite hard. If powdered ferromanganese be added to molten iron in the proportion of about 1 pound of ferro-manganese to 600 pounds of iron, and it is thoroughly diffused through the metal by stirring it with a rod, it will soften hard iron. In some grades of iron such treatment increases the transverse strength of the iron, but when castings that have been subjected to this treatment are remelted, the manganese disappears in the slag, leaving the iron hard.

Manganese has a great affinity for sulphur and can often eliminate it almost wholly from iron by carrying it into the slag. For this reason soft castings may often be made from iron high in manganese when it is charged with iron high in sulphur, on account of the fact that the sulphur is carried out of the iron by the manganese, both passing into the slag. The loss of manganese may be as much as .2 per cent. in a single melting.

Manganese gives life to molten iron, and when ferromanganese as a powder or in small pieces is thrown into iron, it may often act as a physic to purify it and drive out sulphur, a slight odor of sulphur fumes being observed, thus reducing the chance of blowholes existing in castings. Charging moderately high-manganese pig, 1 to 1.5 per cent., in the cupola gives better results, actually carrying the impurities off in the slag, and is more economical than using ferromanganese either in the cupola or the ladle.

43. Phosphorus is an element derived from the ores, the flux, and the fuel. When phosphorus is once absorbed by iron it cannot easily be eliminated. Its tendency is to increase in percentage every time iron is remelted. The amount of this increase will depend on the amount of phosphorus in the fuel, as very little of it escapes absorption by

the iron.   In general, phosphorus weakens iron more than
any other of the elements that commonly occur in cast iron.
When over .7 per cent. of phosphorus occurs in castings, it
has a tendency to make them cold-short, or brittle, when
cold.   It surpasses all other elements in increasing the fluidity of molten iron.   High phosphorus with high silicon
produces an extremely fluid iron, but it has very little
strength.   Necessity for extra fluidity or life in molten iron
is about the only good reason that can be given for allowing
phosphorus to exceed 1 per cent. in iron castings requiring
any strength.   Phosphorus increases the fusibility of iron,
and hence for castings required to stand high temperatures,
it is best to keep the percentage of phosphorus as low as
practical.   Malleable iron must be low in phosphorus.

44. Phosphorus greatly counteracts the tendency of
sulphur to increase combined carbon, shrinkage, contraction, and chill.   Where high sulphur is giving trouble by
causing hard castings, if there is no other practical remedy
at hand, the evil may often be overcome by increasing the
phosphorus from .25 per cent. to .4 per cent.   Each .1 per
cent. increase of phosphorus in iron will, in many cases,
give about the same results physically in counteracting the
effect of sulphur that an increase of .25 per cent. of silicon
will give, where all the other elements remain constant.
By using phosphorus instead of silicon to counteract the
effects of sulphur and soften the iron, the fluidity of the
iron is much increased, all the gases and dross can easily
come to the surface, and the castings are more free from
blowholes and shrink holes than if silicon had been used.
In a general way, where castings are not subjected to high
temperatures, .2 per cent. to .7 per cent. of phosphorus in
iron assists in the production of good castings by making
the iron flow better.

45.   Aluminum is rarely found in pig iron, and has to
be alloyed with it, either in a pure form or alloyed with
other metals.   It is added to iron by placing it in the bottom of the ladle and allowing the iron to flow over it, or by

throwing it on the surface of the molten iron, the first being the better plan. In either case the mixture should be well stirred. The influences of aluminum are similar to those of silicon, the latter being cheaper. Where the combined carbon is high, aluminum will lower it so as to make the iron softer. Where the percentage of graphitic carbon is high, aluminum will close the grain, give the iron a leaden color, and generally decrease the strength, except in cases where the graphitic carbon exceeds the limit that affords iron the greatest strength. As a rule, aluminum will only increase the strength of very hard grades of iron, or those containing 1.4 to 1.8 per cent. combined carbon. The amount of aluminum used in iron varies from .25 per cent. to 1.25 per cent. It will increase the fluidity of hard grades of iron, but generally causes soft grades to be sluggish with an excessive amount of dross on the surface, in this latter respect being similar to silicon. When pouring castings from iron containing aluminum by means of two ladles, cold-shuts are liable to occur at the places where the flowing streams meet. On the whole, aluminum and iron make a very erratic alloy, which may work contrary to expectations.

46. **Titanium** is found in many brands of foundry and Bessemer iron, running from a trace up to .1 per cent. Owing to the fact that ores high in titanium are difficult to smelt and cause much trouble in the furnace, they are avoided as far as possible. It increases the strength of iron very materially, but its other qualities are not known. Ferrotitanium is now being made and gives promise of becoming useful in some mixtures.

47. **Nickel.**—Iron has a strong affinity for **nickel.** Of the 550 meteorites of which there is any record, in all that contain iron, nickel is invariably present, in a few cases being as high as 40 per cent. Nickel imparts wonderful properties to iron through its peculiar effect on the carbon contained. Steel having under .25 per cent. of carbon has its ductility and tensile strength greatly increased by the addition of from 3 to 6 per cent. of nickel.

48. Loss of Iron by Oxidation in Melting.—There is always more or less iron lost by oxidation in the cupola. The larger the amount of surface exposed to the action of the blast and the stronger its pressures, also the thicker the scale of rust or dirt on the iron, the greater will be the loss from this cause.

In a series of experiments on this subject, the following facts were developed: Sandless or chilled pig iron was the least affected, showing a loss of from 3 to 4 per cent. Sand pig iron, fairly cleaned from loose sand, showed a loss of from 4 to 5 per cent. Scrap-iron plate ranging from $1\frac{1}{2}$ to 3 inches thick showed a loss of from 5 to 7 per cent. Scrap plate ranging from $\frac{1}{2}$ to 1 inch thick showed a loss of from 6 to 8 per cent. With fairly clean stove plate the loss ran from 12 to 20 per cent. Burned iron and tin-sheet plate, called *tin scrap*, showed a loss ranging from 25 per cent. up to nothing but slag. A high bed and a strong blast will cause a greater loss than a low bed of fuel and a mild blast. There will be more *shot iron*, i. e., iron more or less globular in form, such as the drippings from the foundry ladle, etc., coming from a low bed of fuel than a high one, for the reason that the latter will melt the cleaner at the close of a heat and will leave less refuse sticking to the sides of the cupola to be carried down by the dump. If a low bed is used, the iron should be carefully picked from the cinder to avoid unnecessary loss. There is also a loss of iron in the slag, depending on the pressure of the blast and the size of the slag hole. By investigating the losses in the slag and from oxidation, and studying their causes, it will generally be possible to operate the cupola so as to reduce them.

MELTING POINT OF CAST IRON.

49. It is often necessary to melt several different mixtures in one heat, and to do this, it is necessary to know which class of iron will melt first. If two radically different grades of iron are charged together, and one melts sooner than the other and is drawn off first and poured, the result will not be the mixture expected. When it is desired to charge a hard grade of iron, to be followed by a soft one, or vice versa, it is very important to know the different melting points of the various brands so as to keep the irons separate. In most cases it is not necessary to know at what temperature the different brands of iron melt, but simply to know which melts first.

50. Comparing Melting Points of Cast Iron.—In order to determine or compare the melting points of various brands of iron, a series of experiments were made by two foundry experts. The tests of one were made in an assaying furnace, converted for the time into a cupola, while the tests of the other were made in the twin-shaft cupola illustrated in Fig. 1. The results of both, although made under different conditions and independently, agreed in showing that it required a higher temperature to melt soft gray iron than hard, chilled, or white iron, and that the latter will melt faster than the former; also, that scrap steel requires a higher temperature than do soft grades of cast iron. The assaying furnace was arranged so that a Le Chatelier pyrometer could be used to record the temperatures. Table III shows the results of tests on six samples.

TABLE III.

MELTING POINTS OF DIFFERENT BRANDS OF IRON.

Combined Carbon. Percentage.	Graphitic Carbon. Percentage.	Character of Fracture.	Melting Point. Degrees F.	Remarks.
1.60	3.16	Gray	2,210	{ Samples cast
4.67	.03	White	2,000	from same ladle.
1.57	2.90	Gray	2,250	{ Samples cast
4.20	.20	White	1,990	from same ladle.
1.20	2.90	Gray	2,250	{ Samples cast
3.90	.16	White	2,000	from same ladle.

These samples were obtained from the same ladle by pouring some of the metal into chills, shown in Fig. 2 (*a*), thus forming chilled castings about $2\frac{1}{4}$ inches in diameter by 6 inches long, as shown at (*b*), and some of the metal into sand molds, formed with a pattern of the same size as the chilled casting. In melting these samples, the chilled iron was placed on one side *e*, and the gray

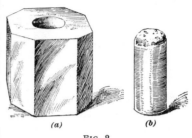

(*a*)   (*b*)

FIG. 2.

iron, or that unchilled, on the other side *f*, of the cupola shown in Fig. 1. As the conditions on the two sides of this cupola are practically alike, it is evident that the sample of iron that melts first must have the lower melting point and will come down first in a regular cupola.

51. Important Observations in Melting Cast Iron.—During the melting of 73 specimens, the following actions were observed: The white irons held their shape, the iron running from the sides and bottom freely, leaving smooth surfaces. The gray irons became soft and dropped in lumps, leaving a ragged surface. Ferromanganese became soft and mushy, exhibiting a consistency of putty before finally running down. Ferrotungsten behaved in the most marked way. As it melted, it acted like white iron, but instead of chilling quickly, it ran through the coke, coming down the spout in thin streams like quicksilver, and collected in a pool in the pan of sand. Both experimenters concluded that the higher the combined carbon, independent of the amount of graphitic carbon present, the lower the melting point.

The temperatures at which different brands of iron actually melt, however, have but little to do with the temperatures to which the metal must be raised before it can be poured into molds. While it is true that white iron will melt at a lower temperature than gray iron, the fact must not be overlooked that white iron must have a higher temperature than gray iron to be poured into the same class of castings, on account of the fact that white iron chills in the ladle or gates of the mold much more quickly than gray iron.

SPECIFICATIONS FOR FOUNDRY PIG IRON.

52. General Requirements for Foundry Irons. Founding establishments making their mixtures often purchase all materials according to specifications, based on their composition as shown by chemical analysis. Standards have been developed for each style of castings and for the methods of making the analyses. Aside from the percentages of metalloids, it is specified for all brands that they be of good, clean iron, free as possible from dross, kish, oxide, sand, etc., and that the percentage of sows must not vary to any great extent from the usual amount found in a strictly graded iron. The following specifications are taken from standard practice. Explanations regarding the action and influence of the various metalloids are given in detail elsewhere under their respective headings. The following chemical methods are used in making the analyses called for in these specifications, the standardized drillings furnished by the American Foundrymen's Association being used as standards to check the chemical work: for silicon, Drown's method; for sulphur, evolution and titration with iodine (volumetric) as a rapid method, and the oxidation method (gravimetric) in all cases of dispute; for phosphorus, Emmerton's method for rapid work, and the molybdate-magnesia method for accurate determinations; for manganese, Deshay's or the colorimetric method for rapid work, and the acetate process for extremely accurate work; carbons are worked by the colorimetric and combustion methods, and in cases of dispute, check analyses are made by gravimetric methods. A carload is taken as the unit for sampling pig iron. The analyses of the different grades of pig iron are given in Table IV.

TABLE IV.

SPECIFICATIONS FOR PIG IRON.

Class of Iron.	Silicon. Preferred. Per Cent.	Silicon. Not Less Than. Per Cent.	Silicon. Not To Exceed. Per Cent.	Sulphur. Must Not Exceed. Per Cent.	Phosphorus. Must Not Exceed. Per Cent.	Phosphorus. Should Not Exceed. Per Cent.	Phosphorus. Not Less Than. Per Cent.	Manganese. Not Less Than. Per Cent.	Manganese. Should Not Exceed. Per Cent.	Manganese. Preferred. Per Cent.	Total Carbon. Maximum. Per Cent.	Total Carbon. Minimum. Per Cent.	Total Carbon. Not Specified.
No. 1 foundry	See Art. 52	2.50		.030		.60		.3	.5	See Art. 52	4.50	3.0	See Art. 52
No. 2 foundry		1.95		.040		.70		.2	.7		4.20	2.9	
No. 3 foundry		1.35		.050		.80		.9	.9		4.00	2.4	
Silicon pig		3.00	5.50	.040		.90		.3	3.0		3.00	2.5	
Ferrosilicon pig		7.00	12.00	.040		.70		.6	2.5			.5	
Manganese pig		2.50		.040					1.2				
Malleable Bessemer, common		.70	2.10	.045	.15						3.75		
Malleable Bessemer, straight		1.00	1.50	.040	.10								
Charcoal iron		.30		.025	.25			.3	.7		4.50	2.5	
Phosphoric pig		1.50	2.75	.055			1		.9			3.0	

53. No. 1 Foundry Pig Iron.—The total carbon will usually be between 3 and 4.5 per cent. in **No. 1 foundry pig iron.** Any car of this iron that shows on analysis less than 2.4 per cent. silicon or more than .035 per cent. sulphur will be rejected.

54. No. 2 Foundry Pig Iron.—The total carbon in **No. 2 foundry pig iron** will generally range from 2.9 to 4.2 per cent. Any car of this iron that shows on analysis less than 1.85 per cent. silicon or more than .045 per cent. sulphur will be rejected.

55. No. 3 Foundry Pig Iron.—The total carbon in **No. 3 foundry pig iron** will usually be between 2.5 and 4 per cent. Any car of No. 3 foundry iron that shows on analysis less than 1.25 per cent. silicon or more than .055 per cent. sulphur will be rejected.

56. Silver-gray silicon pig iron is to be used as a softener and is expected to be medium high in silicon and not too low in graphitic carbon. Any car showing on analysis less than 3 per cent. of silicon or more than .055 per cent. of sulphur will be rejected.

57. Ferrosilicon Pig Iron.—The specification for **ferrosilicon pig iron** calls for a pig iron with about 8 per cent. silicon, the general range in this grade being from 6 to 12 per cent. As a rule, the graphitic carbon will be low, varying from .5 to 3 per cent. Cars will be rejected that show less than 6 per cent. of silicon or more than .045 per cent. of sulphur.

58. Manganese pig iron calls for an iron having from 1 to 2.5 per cent. manganese, the No. 1 pig iron running about 1.5 per cent. in manganese filling the required conditions. It is an ordinary iron made from ore containing somewhat more manganese than the regular foundry irons and carries from .8 to 3.5 per cent. As a rule, the higher the manganese, the greater the proportion of combined carbon, and this pig is added to the foundry pig mixture to raise the combined carbon and increase the strength. The combined carbon may range from .3 to 3 per cent., and the graphitic carbon from .4 to 3.5 per cent.   In a measure, the manganese pig neutralizes the effect of sulphur, removes excess of gas, and prevents blowholes.   It must be used with caution, as low silicon and carbon with high manganese give hard iron and alter shrinkage.

59. Malleable Bessemer Pig Iron.—The specification is the same as for *common* Bessemer iron, as given in Art. **21.**   As a rule, the combined carbon will vary from .3 to 1.3 per cent., and the graphitic carbon from 3.45 to 1.8 per cent.   When the preferred percentages are stated, an iron not varying more than .1 per cent. either way is expected.   When no preferred figures are given, the silicon and manganese may be anywhere within the prescribed limits.

When the *straight* Bessemer is specified, the phosphorus is not to exceed .1 per cent., with from 1 to 1.5 per cent. silicon, about .6 per cent. manganese, and less than .04 per cent. sulphur.   Iron for these grades will be rejected if the analysis shows more than .05 per cent. sulphur or more than .18 per cent. phosphorus.

60. Charcoal iron differs from coke iron mainly in regard to the carbon.   The graphitic carbon appears to be in a finer state of division, and when changed into the combined form, it produces a closer grain and stronger metal than does a coke iron having the same total carbon.   It is especially adapted to chill work, almost any desired chill being obtained by regulating the amount of silicon and carbon.   The sulphur, phosphorus, and manganese are nearly constant in charcoal iron; silicon and carbon vary greatly and govern the various grades.

Graded according to fracture, there are usually seven grades, designated by letters and numbers, and as *soft*, *foundry*, *medium*, *high carbon*, *low carbon*, etc.   Low carbon approximates 2.5 per cent.; medium, 3.5 per cent.; and high, 4.5 per cent., or over.

61. Phosphoric pig iron is used almost exclusively for small, thin castings where great fluidity is desired, it being essential in this work to fill all parts of the mold with a clear, solid casting. Any car showing on analysis more than .06 per cent. sulphur or less than .9 per cent. phosphorus will be rejected.

Table IV gives the metalloid percentages required in the ten grades of pig iron just given.

62. Scrap Iron.—This term is used to designate that large product which has been remelted one or more times, and consists of castings that have been in service, and also the gates, defective castings, etc. in the shop, which must be utilized in new work. As outside scrap costs less than pig iron, the greatest possible amount is used in cupola mixtures. On the other hand, scrap is so variable that it is not proper to use it in special mixtures.

One great difference between scrap iron and pig iron lies in the fact that the former permits experienced persons to define its grade by the appearance of its fracture much better than is possible with pig iron. Generally, castings are allowed to cool under conditions that do not permit the great variations in the grain of the metal that occur in pig iron; also, the form of the casting in which the iron is found is some guide as to its grade.

With a little experience in grading scrap iron, one should be able to decide quite accurately how hard or soft the iron will become when remelted. As a rule, it is impracticable to make a chemical analysis of scrap iron, on account of the fact that it comes to the founder's yard in no regular order or system. A pile of scrap iron is more liable to come from a dozen different kinds of castings made in different parts of the country than from one heat or mixture, and it is next to impossible to get a fair sample for analysis. Almost any intelligent laborer should, with a little training, be able to select and pile up scrap according to its grade in a more economical and practical manner than can be done by attempting to analyze it.

63. Grading Scrap Iron.—A good plan in classifying scrap iron is to adopt a system of grades to be defined by numbers, as in grading pig iron. In order to obtain a standard of grades to compare scrap iron, one may adopt the texture and grain that will be obtained by the remelting of pig iron, containing, before being charged, 1, 2, and 3 per cent. of silicon, respectively, with sulphur supposed to be constant at .03 per cent., and the phosphorus and manganese as generally found in the character of pig iron being used. With such a system, one should soon learn to recognize the fracture of castings from such mixtures of pig iron when poured into castings ranging from the thickness of stove plate upwards to bodies 4 inches or 6 inches thick, and also to pick out the corresponding grades in the scrap iron. As an approximate guide to the sulphur and silicon contents of gray scrap, it can be said that iron ranging from stove plate up to 1 inch in thickness may be considered as an approximate equivalent of remelted pig iron in which the silicon ranged from 2 per cent. down to 1.5 per cent., and for bodies from 1 inch to 3 inches thick, from 1.75 per cent. down to 1 per cent. silicon, sulphur in all cases to be considered as constant at about .06 per cent. Above 3 inches in thickness, an open, gray fracture can range in silicon, with scrap iron, all the way from 2 per cent. down to .75 per cent. The grading of such heavy bodies generally requires more skill than is necessary with light and medium thicknesses of scrap iron, but practice should soon enable one to guess fairly close in judging the grade of heavy or thick bodies as well as light ones. In cases where scrap iron comes to the founder's yard in the form of complete castings that have to be broken, he can, by sizing up the general proportions of the whole casting, judge much closer the grade in the massive parts than if the scrap iron were received in a miscellaneous broken condition mixed with other irons. One of the most difficult classes of scrap to pass judgment on as to its grade is white iron. In castings ranging from the thickness of stove plate up to 2 inches, the silicon may range all the way from 1.5 per cent. down to .5 per cent.

In castings over 3 inches thick, it is generally safe to con-
clude, if the section is all white, that the silicon can range
from .4 per cent. down to .1 per cent., with sulphur in any
of these thicknesses ranging all the way from .05 per cent.
to .2 per cent. As a rule, it can be taken for granted that
the sulphur is very high and the silicon very low in all scrap
iron having an entirely white fracture.

It is almost impossible to pass judgment on the analyses
of burned iron, especially if badly burned. As a rule, such
iron is unsuited for any work other than that of making
castings similar to sash weights. When scrap iron exceeds
one-half of the mixture, it is customary to allow the mixer
a leeway of .1 to .15 per cent. on silicon and .005 to .01 per
cent. on sulphur.

64. Method of Using Scrap Iron.—All founders
have more or less fine scrap and shot iron collected from the
shop's refuse and cupola dumps that should be remelted.
Such refuse can be used, a few shovelfuls at a time, by
evenly distributing it over the top of the regular charge in
the cupola. Manufacturers of very light small-work castings
find the most difficulty in utilizing their shop's refuse. In
some cases the fine shot, etc., is held until the last of the
heat and utilized for a few heavy castings, the rest being
poured into pig beds.

Care should be taken to have all the scrap as free from
scale or dirt as possible. Some founders go so far as to
tumble all gates and sprues before charging them, so as to
avoid dirt in the iron. Just as much care and judgment
should be exercised in the selection of scrap as in selecting
pig iron, if good results and success are desired.

65. Specifications for Machinery Scrap. — The
specifications for scrap iron vary to some extent according
to the class of castings to be made. For use in the manufacture of agricultural implements and light machinery,
there is required a good clean scrap from similar castings,
free from excess of rust. When a car of scrap is received,
the inspector should superintend the unloading and discard

the following objectionable pieces: Wrought iron, steel, burned stove plate, grate bars, car wheels, brake shoes, large chilled work, burned malleables, and large pieces weighing more than 400 pounds.

66. Proportioning Iron Mixtures.—It is not always possible to obtain pig iron having the exact composition desired for the castings, and hence it is necessary to determine the percentages of the elements in the resulting product when two or more brands of iron are melted together or to select the proper amounts of different brands to make the desired composition. As a rule, the furnaceman only guarantees to keep the phosphorus and manganese within certain limits in the iron he furnishes, silicon and sulphur being allowed to vary to much wider limits. Iron undergoes other changes in a cupola besides being melted. There is a loss of from .2 to .3 per cent. in silicon and from .1 to .5 per cent. in manganese, and there may be variations in the other metalloids, so that allowance must be made for these after the theoretical percentages have been determined. The method of making these computations will be best understood from practical examples, taking silicon as the element under consideration. It is required to make a mixture containing 3 per cent. of silicon from two brands of pig iron containing 3.4 per cent. and 2.8 per cent. silicon, respectively. Every 100 pounds of mixture is to contain 3 pounds of silicon. Of the individual brands, 100 pounds of the first contains 3.4, and the second 2.8, pounds of silicon. Hence, one brand has .4 pound too much and the other .2 pound too little silicon. The problem then is to determine the amounts of each to use so that the excess of one will balance the deficiency of the other, and then to make a proper allowance for loss in the cupola. For a mixture running from 3 to 4 per cent., or over, in silicon, the loss may be as much as 20 per cent. By this is meant the ratio of the loss in silicon to the original amount; thus, if the contents were 5 per cent. and the loss 20 per cent., or one-fifth of this, the net amount in the casting would be 4 per cent.

Continuing with the example, and taking 100 pounds of mixture for a basis, if the pounds of high-silicon pig (H. S. P.) be multiplied by the percentage of silicon contained, the product will be the amount of silicon in pounds in it; likewise, if the low-silicon pig (L. S. P.) be multiplied by the percentage of silicon contained, the product will be the amount of silicon in pounds in it. Not allowing for losses, it is desired that the proportions of the two grades be such that the sum of these two products equals 3 pounds of silicon. This computation may be summarized as follows:

Pounds high-silicon pig $\times$ .034 + pounds low-silicon pig $\times$ .028 = 100 $\times$ .03 = 3 pounds silicon. But as the iron mixture is to weigh 100 pounds, the pounds of low-silicon iron (L. S. I.) is equal to 100 pounds minus the pounds of high-silicon iron (H. S. I.), and the statement may be written thus:

Pounds H. S. I. $\times$ .034 + (100 pounds − pounds H. S. I.) $\times$ .028 = 3 pounds; or, .034 H. S. I. + 100 $\times$ .028 − .028 H. S. I. = 3; or, .006 H. S. I. + 2.8 = 3; or, .006 H. S. I. = 3. − 2.8 = .2; or, H. S. I. = .2 ÷ .006 = $33\frac{1}{3}$ pounds; and the L. S. I. = 100 − $33\frac{1}{3}$ = $66\frac{2}{3}$ pounds. This shows that the mixture must be made up of one-third high-silicon iron and two-thirds low-silicon iron; and if the casting requires 1,500 pounds of metal, 500 pounds of H. S. I. and 1,000 pounds of L. S. I. must be charged into the cupola, no allowance being made in this example for losses.

67. Rule for Proportioning Iron Mixtures.—*From the number representing the greater percentage take the number representing the required percentage and multiply the remainder by 100, which gives the number of pounds of the brand of iron containing the smaller percentage that is to be used in the mixture. From the required percentage take the smaller percentage and multiply the remainder by 100; this will give the number of pounds of the brand of iron containing the greater percentage to be used in the mixture.*

EXAMPLE.—If a founder has two brands of iron, one of which contains .75 per cent. of silicon and the other 1.75 per cent. of silicon, and he desires to make a mixture containing 1 per cent. of silicon, what proportion of each brand should be used in the mixture?

SOLUTION.—Applying the rule just given, we get $(1.75 - 100) \times 100 = 75$ lb. of iron containing the smaller percentage of silicon, and $(1.00 - .75) \times 100 = 25$ lb. of iron containing the larger percentage of silicon, as the amounts to be used in the mixture. Since the amounts are in the proportion of 25 to 75, or 1 to 3, it follows that 3 parts of the iron containing the smaller percentage of silicon should be used for every part of the other iron.

68. Allowance for Loss of Silicon in Melting. Suppose the loss in silicon in melting is 20 per cent. of the amount charged (A. C.), then the computations in the preceding example must be modified to conform to actual practice. If the charge contains 10 pounds of silicon, and 20 per cent. is lost, then the casting will contain 10 pounds minus 20 per cent. of 10 pounds, which may be stated as follows:

$$10 - (10 \times .20) = 10 - 2 = 8.$$

Now if 8 pounds are required, to find the amount to be charged, the process is reversed as follows: The pounds to be charged must equal 8 pounds plus 20 per cent. of the amount charged; hence, amount charged $= 8 +$ amount charged $\times .20$; or, A. C. $- .20$ A. C. $= 8$; or, $.8$ A. C. $= 8$; or, A. C. $= 8 \div .8 = 10$.

Applying this principle to a mixture of 100 pounds and making the estimate to allow for 20 per cent. loss of the silicon, the statement may be written as follows, when it is desired to have 3 per cent. of silicon in the casting: A. C. $- .2$ A. C. $= 3$; or, $.8$ A. C. $= 3$; or, A. C. $= 3 \div .8 = 3.75$ pounds of silicon required in the charge of 100 pounds of pig iron.

69. Rule for Loss of Silicon in Melting.—*To find the number of pounds of any metalloid to be charged into the cupola to allow for a definite loss, divide the amount to be in the casting by 1 less the loss per unit.*

The number of pounds to be used of each brand of iron in the mixture is next to be determined. As the required silicon is above the contents of the higher-silicon iron used in the example, Art. **67,** it is necessary to use a still higher grade for this particular mixture. Suppose 6-per-cent.-silicon pig is available, then the computations for the proportions are as follows: $(6 - 3.75) \times 100 = 225$, and $(3.75 - 3.4) \times 100 = 35$. The sum of these numbers is 260, and the proportions are $\frac{225}{260}$ and $\frac{35}{260}$, or $\frac{45}{52}$ and $\frac{7}{52}$; that is, 45 pounds of the low-silicon pig must be used for each 7 pounds of the high-silicon pig. If, for example, the cupola charge requires 5,200 pounds of iron, then the number of pounds of low-silicon pig is equal to $\frac{5,200}{45+7} \times 45 = \frac{5,200}{52} \times 45 = 100 \times 45 = 4,500$; and the pounds of high-silicon iron is $5,200 - 4,500 = 700$.

The work may be proved as follows: $700 \times .06 = 42 =$ the number of pounds of silicon in the 6-per-cent. pig used; and $4,500 \times .034 = 153$ pounds of silicon in the 3.4-per-cent. pig, making a total of $42 + 153 = 195$ pounds of silicon in the charge. If 20 per cent. of this is lost, there remains 156 pounds, and this is equal to 3 per cent. of 5,200, as required in the casting.

The application of the rule is made in the same manner to get the proportions for any weight of mixture or for any element.

MIXTURES OF CAST IRON.

70. Examples of Iron Mixtures.—Those mixing iron by analysis usually have a preference for certain combinations, and naturally use mixtures giving the best results under existing conditions. For example, if the castings are to be cooled slowly or partly annealed, the silicon is generally made as low as possible, or to a point where extreme hardness does not interfere with machining.

The examples of mixtures for specific castings given in Tables V and VI are from current practice in foundry work. Table V gives a mixture for disappearing-gun mounts, which

TABLE V.

IRON FOR DISAPPEARING-GUN MOUNTS.

Class of Iron.	Percentage in Mixture.
No. 3 Muirkirk charcoal iron......	5 to 15
No. 4½ Muirkirk charcoal iron......	3½ to 15
No. 4 high Landon charcoal iron...	25 to 30
No. 4 low Landon charcoal iron....	30
Gun-iron scrap....................	20 to 25

was melted in the cupola at the Niles Tool Works, Hamilton, Ohio, and gave a tensile strength of about 33,000 pounds per square inch with an elongation of from .5 to .6 per cent. The percentages of metalloids in this mixture are given in Table VI; the table also gives the percentages in several mixtures used for specific purposes. The car-wheel iron of Table VI had stood hard service for from 8 to 11 years. It was made from both charcoal and coke irons, the percentage being from average analyses. The gray-iron mixture for hard, strong, close-grained iron for ammonia cylinders shows considerable variation in the elements. Where the castings are allowed to cool slowly, or are annealed, the silicon should not be over 1.6 per cent.; if not annealed, it may be from 1.6 to 1.9 per cent. The sulphur may run to .15 per cent. only where there is a high total carbon, though it is better to keep it lower on account of excessive shrinkage. Phosphorus should be kept below .7 per cent., and if greater strength is required, .4 per cent. or less is better. The manganese is made as high as .8 per cent. only in cases of high sulphur. In mixing the medium iron for engine cylinders and gears, 1.5 per cent. silicon gives the best results for gears and 1.6 per cent. for cylinders. If the castings have thin parts, or are not cooled slowly, add .10 to .20 per cent. of silicon. Sulphur is best kept below .085 per cent., but if the manganese is over .6 per cent., the sulphur may run up to .1 per cent. The phosphorus should not exceed .7 per cent. The ideal soft mixture for pulleys and small castings has 2.4 per cent. silicon, with sulphur not above .085 per cent. Phosphorus may go to the limit of .95 per cent. in thin castings, but if strength is wanted, it is best to keep it below .7 per cent. Manganese gives the best results when between .4 and .6 per cent.

TABLE VI.

CHEMICAL ANALYSES OF IRON MIXTURES.

Class of Iron.	Silicon.	Sulphur.	Manganese.	Phosphorus.	Combined Carbon.	Graphitic Carbon.	Total Carbon.
Chill roll............	.84	.071	.285	.547	.61	2.45	3.06
Gun metal.........	.73	.059	.408	.453	.76	2.47	3.23
Car wheel.........	.78	.132	.306	.364	1.07	2.36	3.43
General machinery.	1.30	.053	.224	.433	.58	3.31	3.89
Stove plate........	2.47	.094	.265	.508	.19	4.00	4.19
Bessemer iron......	1.52	.059	.326	.083	.49	3.73	4.22
Mixture of Table V.	1.00	.050	.600	.300	1.10	1.40	2.50
Car wheels in hard service 8 to 11 years...........	.58 to .68	.050 to .080	.150 to .270	.250 to .450	.63 to 1.01	2.56 to 3.10	3.19 to 4.11
Ammonia cylinders	1.20 to 1.90	.095 to .150	.800 to .600	.400 to .700			
Engine cylinders, gears, etc., medium iron.......	1.40 to 2.00	.085 to .100	.300 to .700	.700			
Pulleys, small castings, etc., soft iron...........	2.2 to 2.8	.085 to .070	.300 to .700	.700 to .950			

71. Mixtures for Soft Castings.—The first thing to be done in making iron mixtures is to decide on the physical qualities that are desired in the castings. If only a common grade of castings is required, a mixture can be made by taking one-third of No. 1 foundry pig iron and two-thirds of scrap iron. The No. 1 pig should run from 2.75 per cent. to 3 per cent. in silicon; sulphur, from .01 per cent. to .03 per cent.; manganese, .3 per cent. to .6 per cent.; and phosphorus, .25 per cent. to .5 per cent. The scrap to go with the mixture should range in silicon 1.5 per cent. to 2.5 per cent., and sulphur, .05 per cent. to .08 per cent. Such a mixture should be soft enough to machine in castings over 1 inch thick.

If the castings are to be thinner than 1 inch, the percentage of scrap should be decreased. For castings about ¼ inch thick, a mixture of about three-fourths pig and one-fourth scrap will be required.

For light small castings and stove-plate work, a pig ranging from 3.5 per cent. to 3.75 per cent. in silicon, and not over .02 per cent. in sulphur, and manganese from .3 per cent. to .5 per cent., with phosphorus .7 per cent. to 1 per cent., should work well. The carbon in the foundry irons should not be less than 3.25 per cent., and higher if practicable up to 4 per cent.

Ferrosilicon containing 5 to 6 per cent. of silicon can often be mixed with 80-per-cent. scrap, running from 1.5 per cent. to 2 per cent. in silicon, and the castings finish fairly well when above 1 inch in thickness. When using ferrosilicon where it runs 4 per cent. or above in silicon, great care must be exercised to get just the amount necessary, for if too much is used, it may render the castings so brittle and weak that they will crack on the least jar.

It is always well to use iron from two or more furnaces in all mixtures, on account of the fact that this reduces the effect of any irregularities existing in one grade of iron that, if used by itself, could injure the mixture. In the manufacture of some specialties, as stove plate and light hardware, it is necessary to use all pig iron, no scrap being permitted in the mixture, except that coming from gates, defective castings, etc.

72. Mixtures for Hard and Chilled Castings. The silicon in pig iron for such work as chilled rolls, car wheels, and other classes of chilled castings generally ranges from .5 to 1.25 per cent., with the sulphur, manganese, and phosphorus varying according to the specialty being manufactured. The character of the chill often has more to do with the durability of chilled work than its depth. A chill promoted chiefly by manganese will be found better able to yield to stresses, and not so liable to crack on the surface of castings (which is done at the moment of solidification), or from *heat wear* in use (as in the case of rolling-mill rolls), than a chill that is chiefly promoted by sulphur, although manganese is best and often necessary to enable the wheels to stand the thermal test. For *friction wear*, as in the case of the tread of car wheels or brake shoes, a chill produced by sulphur gives more life than one produced by manganese. The temperature and fluidity of the metal with which a casting is poured, as well as the thickness of the casting, all have an influence on the depth of chilling. A casting poured with hot iron will chill deeper than one poured with dull iron, and a heavy casting will chill less than a light one in all cases where the thickness of the iron mold or chill used is about the same.

For making chilled castings, charcoal iron is generally used, although the use of coke and anthracite iron is increasing, especially since it has become the practice to select iron by analysis. In making mixtures for some kinds of chilled work, a fair percentage of scrap iron may be mixed with pig iron. The scrap generally used in mixtures for chilled work consists of chilled castings, such as chilled rolls, car wheels, brake shoes, and plow points. In judging the grade of chilled scrap, the gray body as well as the chilled portion of the iron should be considered. The pouring of the castings with a hot or a dull iron makes a difference in the depth of the chill that might deceive one in judging its grade, if no

note were taken of both the gray body and the chilled
portions.

73. Remelting Chilled Iron. — Foundrymen were
formerly in the habit of picking out the chilled portions of
castings and using them only for extremely low-grade work,
such as sash weights, etc., but a series of experiments with
this kind of iron seems to prove that it is softened by remelting. In the experiment, the chilled parts of the scrap iron
were separated from the gray parts and both melted sepa-
rately, and the castings from the chilled scrap were softer
than those from the gray scrap. When chilled iron contains
the requisite amount of total carbon, remelting will often
transform a sufficient amount of the carbon to the graphitic
form to produce a very good soft gray iron. Owing to the
fact that chilled castings are generally made from high-
grade irons, it is evident that this chilled scrap can often be
used in the very best foundry mixtures, especially in the
case where the chilled scrap is composed of castings made
from good charcoal iron low in sulphur. This is on account
of the fact that the combined carbon in the chilled iron is
freed by remelting, and if allowed to cool slowly, will take
the free or graphitic form. The general character of the
chilled iron can be judged more closely from the gray portion than from the white portion, when selecting scrap for
ordinary foundry mixtures.

**74. Mixing Steel and Wrought Iron With Cast
Iron.** — In making the strongest grades of cast iron, from
15 per cent. to 30 per cent. of scrap steel is sometimes
mixed with the iron. Wrought iron is also used, but, as a
rule, soft grades of steel give the best results. In charging
the steel or wrought iron into a cupola, it is generally mixed
with the cast iron the same as the other scrap, but more
fuel is required on account of their higher melting points.
The strongest steel and iron mixtures are obtained by melting in an air furnace The metal obtained by this process
is called semisteel, and may have a tensile strength of from
40,000 to 50,000 pounds per square inch.

TESTING CAST IRON.

EXPLANATION OF TERMS USED IN TESTING CAST IRON.

75. Density is the mass or quantity of matter in a substance per unit of its volume. The *unit of density* is that of water at 39.1° F. at sea level under the mean pressure of the atmosphere. By a *dense iron* is meant one having a fine, close grain, as distinguished from one having a coarse, open grain. The greater density of the former may cause it to weigh from 50 to 60 pounds more per cubic foot than a coarse-grained iron. A cubic foot of white iron weighs about 475 pounds, and a cubic foot of dark-gray iron 425 pounds.

76. Tenacity is that property by virtue of which a substance resists being pulled apart. The tensile strength of cast iron may vary from 7,000 to 40,000 pounds per square inch, depending on the mixture. Owing to its low ductility, cast iron breaks suddenly under maximum load.

77. Elasticity is that property of matter by virtue of which it tends to return to its normal form or volume when the stress is removed. When it does not so return upon a removal of the load, the material is said to have taken a *permanent set*. The *elastic limit* is the maximum load that can be applied without producing permanent set. In cast iron this is very near the breaking load. For stresses less than the elastic limit, bodies resume their original form upon removal of the load. Good gray cast iron will stretch about $\frac{1}{8}$ inch in every 58 feet per ton tension per square inch up to about one-half the breaking load.

78. Deflection is the divergence or bending from a normal position caused by a stress. The deflection is measured in making transverse tests, also in testing columns. A rough bar of sash-weight iron $\frac{1}{2}$ inch square and 12 inches between supports, when loaded at the middle, will deflect about .06 inch before breaking, while a similar bar of machinery iron will deflect over three times as much.

79. Brittleness and Strength.—Cast iron is said to be **brittle** when it breaks easily. White iron and those high in silicon or phosphorus are usually brittle. Brittle iron should not be used where subjected to sudden loads or jars.

By the **strength** of cast iron is meant its ability to withstand stresses when applied in any of the several ways without yielding or breaking. Tests are usually applied to cast iron transversely and by impact. Cast iron is generally used to resist transverse and crushing stresses, also those from impact or blows. Tensile tests are sometimes used.

80. Chill.—The **chilled** portion of a casting is the hardened skin or shell, in which the greater part or all of the carbon is in the combined form. The term chill is also applied to the metal parts of the mold in contact with the molten iron, and that produce these hardened portions. The chilled structure is white and is produced by suddenly cooling the iron in the surface of the casting in the mold. The chill may be localized in castings by arranging metal parts in the mold, thus carrying off the heat rapidly from certain prescribed areas. Chill is promoted by varying the percentage of sulphur, silicon, manganese, phosphorus, etc. The strength and character of iron depend a great deal on the rate of cooling and thickness of the casting, the time in contact with the chill of the mold, hot iron, rate of contraction, etc.

81. Contraction is that quality of cast iron which causes it to decrease in volume as it cools after solidifying. Contraction depends largely on the form of the casting and its rate of cooling, and may vary greatly in different parts of the same casting, according as to whether the parts are thick or thin. Light bars contract more than heavy ones. The composition also regulates the contraction to a considerable extent. For certain classes of work it is desirable that the iron have as little contraction as possible. This is especially true of those castings not well proportioned. The patternmaker's rule is to allow ⅛ inch per foot for contraction. But this rule must be applied with care to patterns of different proportions. In heavy work the castings may be larger than the patterns. Slow cooling causes less contraction and promotes the formation of more graphitic carbon; hence the casting is more spongy and not so dense.

82. Shrinkage is the term applied to the decrease in volume of cast iron while cooling in a molten state. To overcome shrinkage requires feeding to keep the mold full. It is most noticeable in heavy castings. It also depends on the grade of iron. Cast iron expands at the moment of solidification, a valuable property by virtue of which it takes the exact impression of the mold; then contraction begins, the action being analogous to that of water in its physical changes. This expansion takes place between the actions of shrinkage and contraction. Shrink holes appear in castings near the top, or portions last to solidify, also where light and heavy parts join, the holes being in the latter, or those parts that solidify last. Blow, sand, and dirt holes are different from shrink holes, the former, being formed on both the interior and exterior of the castings, are generally smoother, and are caused by gases not carried away by the vents, or by dirt in the molten iron.

The distinction here made between contraction and shrinkage is one of convenience rather than fact, for the words are generally used as synonyms.

83. Hardness of Cast Iron.—Hardness is a relative term denoting that quality of cast iron the degree of which is determined by its power to scratch or to be scratched by other substances according to an arbitrary scale. Moh's scale of hardness is generally used, and includes ten minerals ranging from talc, the softest, to the diamond, which is the hardest substance known. Practically the hardness of cast iron exhibits itself in the wearing away of the tool used on it. It differs from tenacity in that the latter measures the force to do the cutting and not the wear on the tool.

84. By **stress** is meant the force that acts in the interior of a body and resists the external forces tending to change its form. **Strain** is the deformation or change in form caused by the stress. The stress is measured in pounds per square inch, and the strain in inches. Thus, if a bar of cast iron of 1 square inch section sustains a load of 40,000 pounds and is elongated .55 inch, the stress is 40,000 pounds and the strain is .55 inch.

PHYSICAL TESTS OF CAST IRON.

85. Importance of Physical Tests. — The great number of different brands of cast iron used in the different branches of founding presents very complex problems in mixing. The different grades have radically different characteristics, and these are due not only to differences in chemical composition, but also to the physical condition of the metal. The size and character of the grain in a casting depend largely on the rate of cooling, variations in chemical composition, and the form of the casting. **Physical tests** are those relating to the casting after it is made, and embrace the determination of those practical features most desired by the manufacturer and the consumer, viz., good strength with a close grain; material not too hard to machine; and a shrinkage to correspond with the pattern. In addition to this, the castings are expected to be free from blow and shrink holes, cold shuts, scabby spots, etc. Some of these defects may be eliminated by manipulating the constituents of the mixture, others must be corrected in the molding.

Chemical analysis alone is not a sufficient record of the character of castings. It is necessary to know the physical qualities also. It is necessary to test new brands of iron so as to compare their qualities with those previously used. By using a small cupola, metal for test bars can be easily and cheaply melted and the physical qualities of various mixtures determined. Some founders dispense with test bars and are guided by the analyses and the castings from the iron. This does very well in the manufacture of some forms of

TABLE VII.

TENSILE TESTS OF CAST IRON.

Rough Test Bars Cast in Green Sand.	Percentage of Silicon.	Percentage of Sulphur.	Percentage of Manganese.	Percentage of Phosphorus.	Percentage of Combined Carbon.	Percentage of Graphitic Carbon.	Percentage of Total Carbon.	Dimensions of Cross-Section of Pattern. Inches.	Area of Bar. Square Inches.	Breaking Load. Pounds.	Load in Pounds Per Square Inch.
Soft Bessemer	1.67	.032	.29	.095	.43	3.44	3.87	.5 × .5	0.22	3,620	16,750
Soft Bessemer	1.67	.032	.29	.095	.43	3.44	3.87	.5 × 1	1.09	15,200	13,940
Soft Bessemer	1.67	.032	.29	.095	.43	3.44	3.87	1.5 × 1.5	2.33	29,210	12,530
Soft Bessemer	1.67	.032	.29	.095	.43	3.44	3.87	2 × 2	4.04	44,810	11,110
Soft Bessemer	1.67	.032	.29	.095	.43	3.44	3.87	.56 dia.	.26	4,180	16,090
Soft Bessemer	1.67	.032	.29	.095	.43	3.44	3.87	1.13 dia.	1.00	13,980	13,980
Soft Bessemer	1.67	.032	.29	.095	.43	3.44	3.87	1.69 dia.	2.30	30,580	13,290
Soft Bessemer	1.67	.032	.29	.095	.43	3.44	3.87	2.15 dia.	4.10	47,310	11,540
Dynamo frame iron	1.95	.042	.39	.405	.59	3.23	3.82	.5 × .5	.29	4,920	17,600
Dynamo frame iron	1.95	.042	.39	.405	.59	3.23	3.82	1 × 1	1.01	15,900	15,740
Dynamo frame iron	1.95	.042	.39	.405	.59	3.23	3.82	1.5 × 1	2.24	29,470	13,150
Dynamo frame iron	1.95	.042	.39	.405	.59	3.23	3.82	1.5 × 2	4.02	47,930	11,920
Dynamo frame iron	1.95	.042	.39	.405	.59	3.23	3.82	.56 dia.	.25	4,410	17,640
Dynamo frame iron	1.95	.042	.39	.405	.59	3.23	3.82	1.13 dia.	1.00	15,870	15,870
Dynamo frame iron	1.95	.042	.39	.405	.59	3.23	3.82	1.69 dia.	2.26	29,700	13,140
Dynamo frame iron	1.95	.042	.39	.405	.59	3.23	3.82	2.15 dia.	4.03	47,040	11,670
Light machinery iron	2.04	.044	.39	.578	.32	3.52	3.84	.5 × .5	.25	4,740	18,960
Light machinery iron	2.04	.044	.39	.578	.32	3.52	3.84	1 × 1	1.03	16,360	15,880
Light machinery iron	2.04	.044	.39	.578	.32	3.52	3.84	1.5 × 1.5	2.25	29,260	13,030
Light machinery iron	2.04	.044	.39	.578	.32	3.52	3.84	2 × 2	4.01	45,020	11,210
Light machinery iron	2.04	.044	.39	.578	.32	3.52	3.84	.56 dia.	.25	4,666	18,640
Light machinery iron	2.04	.044	.39	.578	.32	3.52	3.84	1.13 dia.	1.00	16,420	16,420
Light machinery iron	2.04	.044	.39	.578	.32	3.52	3.84	1.69 dia.	2.25	32,470	14,430
Light machinery iron	2.04	.044	.39	.578	.32	3.52	3.84	2.15 dia.	4.06	49,570	12,210

Chemical Composition columns: Silicon, Sulphur, Manganese, Phosphorus, Combined Carbon, Graphitic Carbon, Total Carbon.

castings, for in some cases every casting serves the purpose of a test bar, on account of the fact that if the iron possesses any irregularities, they will be displayed in the casting itself much more quickly than in an ordinary test bar.

Under certain conditions the shrinkage of a test bar varies inversely as the percentage of silicon contained. Hence shrinkage tests are frequently useful. Shrinkage tests are cheaply and rapidly made, and their use is within the scope of small foundries. The strength of a casting is often more dependent on the grain of the iron than on its composition.

86. Actual and Comparative Tests. — Iron for heavy castings generally requires careful physical tests. Test bars do not give the actual strength, construction, and chill of the individual castings. Such information can only be obtained absolutely by making duplicate castings and using one for testing purposes. The test bar gives the relative physical properties of the iron, and from his general knowledge of the properties of this class of iron, the founder can tell quickly from the test bar the qualities of the iron in question. In Table VII is given a series of tensile tests on different forms and sizes of test bars. These tests show that while the three sizes of test bars gave very different values in the individual specimens, they hold about a constant ratio to the strength of the iron, so that a comparison of any one set of bars of the same size throughout the series will give a fair idea of the relative strength of the different brands of iron. Hence, the function of the test bar is to give relative qualities rather than absolute. Physical tests are especially necessary in foundries producing castings such as car wheels, chilled rolls, ingot molds, water pipe, etc.

Frequently test bars are referred to in the specifications by which duplicate castings are ordered. If the chemical composition and physical characteristics of a test bar poured from the same iron from which the original casting was poured are known, it should not be difficult for the founder to produce another casting having practically the same physical characteristics as the first.

87. Size and Form of Test Bars.—The size and form of bars for transverse tests vary greatly, and on this account it is nearly impossible to compare records obtained from different sets of experiments. Both round and square test bars have been used, the length varying from $13\frac{1}{2}$ to 50 inches, and the cross-section from $\frac{1}{2}$ to 5 or 6 square inches. Some of the points that should be observed in selecting the size of a test bar are the following: The test bar should be of such form and size that it will be as little affected by variations in the dampness of the molding sand as possible. In proportion as the molding sand contains moisture, the outside of the bar will receive a greater chilling effect, thus causing more of the carbon to take the combined form and the grain of the bar to be closer. The test bar should also be of such a form that its structure will be uniform throughout, and it should be cast in such a position as to maintain a uniform structure and rate of cooling. Some experimenters claim to have found the round bar very much better than the square one, the reasons for which are given in Art. **88.** One point that should be kept in mind is that the test bar furnishes information that can be used only in the comparison of different mixtures and does not give the ultimate strength of the iron when cast into some other form. From a great many experiments one authority has found that it is not very good practice to use a bar having a sectional area of less than 1 square inch, on account of the fact that variations in the dampness in the sand will greatly affect a small bar. He claims that the small-diameter test bar, having a sectional area of about 1 square inch, is best adapted for soft or medium grades of iron, and that the larger sizes give the best results in the hard grades of iron. Any iron that takes a chill easily requires a large test bar, so that the surface of the bar may bear a smaller relation to the area of the cross-section. The important consideration is to keep the conditions the same in doing the work, so that comparisons can be made that will be useful.

88. Uniform Grain and Structure in Test Bars. Having decided on the dimensions of a test bar, the next

question is how to obtain a uniform structure in it.   If the
square bar is used, as shown in Fig. 3 (*a*), it has been found
that it is surrounded by an outer shell of more dense metal,
as indicated by the shaded portion in the illustration, and

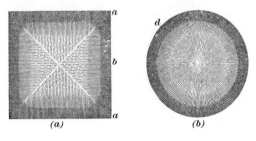

(*a*)   (*b*)

FIG. 3.

that this shell is thicker at the corners *a* than in the center
of the flat surfaces *b*.   It has also been found by careful
analysis that the combined carbon is usually higher at the
corners than at the center, one series of experiments showing that the combined carbon was .134 per cent. higher at
the corners *a* than in the center of the flat surface *b*.   It is
evident from these facts that a uniform structure cannot be
expected from a square bar, no matter in what position it is
cast.

A round bar will also be surrounded by a shell of metal
having a greater density than the central portion of the
casting, as shown in Fig. 3 (*b*), but this outer shell will be
uniform all around the bar, at least in the case of bars cast
on end, and for this reason the round bar cast on end is to
be preferred both for transverse and tension tests.

89. Structure of Test Bars.— In the case of test
bars that are cast flat or on their side, when the load is
applied on the surface that was uppermost in casting, also
designated the *gate* side, a much greater strength is recorded
than when the load is applied on the surface that was at the
bottom during casting.   A careful investigation as to the

structure of bars developed the facts illustrated in Fig. 4. The under surface u will have a thicker outer shell than the upper surface v, and the strength shown by the bar will depend largely on whether this thicker surface is up or down during the test. On this account the test bars should be cast on end. If for any reason it is found necessary to

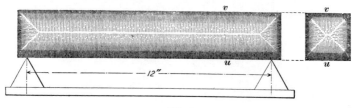

FIG. 4.

cast them horizontally, great care should be taken to see that they are all tested in the same relative position; that is, with the same side uppermost in the testing machine. When test bars are cast horizontally the word *top*, or some character to designate the upper surface of the bar, should be cast on the bar.

A square bar cast horizontally will have more defects, such as blowholes, dirt, etc., than a round bar cast vertically, and its transverse strength is from 200 to 300 pounds greater if broken with the gate side up. Tumbling the bars, either round or square, increases the strength from 100 to 300 pounds.

90. Testing Contraction in Cast Iron.—A knowledge of the contraction of iron will assist the molder greatly in proportioning the parts of a mold and determining whether or not a given brand of iron can safely be poured into the form of a given casting. In designing test bars for determining the contraction, it must be remembered that the contraction is affected more or less by the condition of the molding sand, and for this reason thin or small bars should be avoided. A difference in the moisture of the sand of two molds may make a difference of as much as $\frac{1}{32}$ inch in

12 inches in the contraction of the same brand of iron when using small bars.

One method of measuring the contraction of a test bar of cast iron is to cast the bar between the points *a* and *b* of a yoke *c*, as shown in Fig. 5 (*a*). The yoke *c* is placed in the mold, and a pattern placed between the points *a* and *b*. The yoke is left in the mold during casting, the iron contracting away from it. In the illustration, the casting *e* is shown in place in the same yoke in which it was cast, and

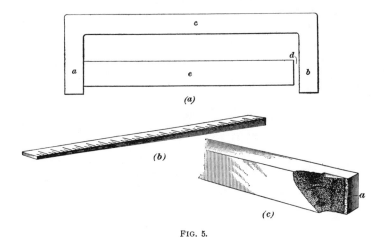

FIG. 5.

the space *d*, between the end of the bar *e* and the end *b* of the yoke *c*, is the contraction of the bar *e*, which may be measured by means of the wedge-shaped scale, shown in Fig. 5 (*b*), in thousandths of an inch per foot. The scale is placed vertically in the space *d*, and the reading made from the graduation on the scale at the top of the test bar.

A method adopted by some founding establishments is to use test bars 1 inch square, cast horizontally in a yoke, having the ends exactly 13.333 inches apart, and to determine both the contraction and the chill in the same mold. The contraction is measured by placing the bar in a laboratory yoke of the same dimensions as the one in which it

was cast and fitted with a micrometer; deducting one-tenth
leaves the contraction per foot. For transverse tests the
bars are laid on supports 12 inches apart, and the load
applied in the middle.

The ends of the bar are cast against a metal chill. After
measuring the contraction as just described, a piece is
broken out of the side of the bar at the end and the depth
of the chill *a* in the test bar, as shown in Fig. 5 (*c*), may be
judged by the eye or measured.

It has been shown that the shrinkage of cast iron depends
more on the influence of silicon than on any other metalloid.
This fact is used in a practical way by some founders to reg-
ulate the shrinkage in their castings. If the test bar gives
a greater shrinkage than desired, they increase the silicon
in the next cast; if less, they decrease the silicon. The
change in the percentage of silicon is accomplished by
the use, in the cupola charge, of scrap iron or of pig iron
containing a different percentage of silicon from that previously used.

91. Comparative Tests of Cast Iron.—Table VIII
gives the results of a series of transverse tests conducted to
determine two points: (1) the comparative strength of different grades of iron; (2) the best size of test bar to use. The
classes of iron tested include those used in making chilled
rolls, gun carriages, car wheels, heavy machinery, stove
plate, and Bessemer-iron castings. The test bars used were
round and of three sizes, the first being $1\frac{1}{8}$ inches, the
second $1\frac{5}{8}$ inches, and the third $1\frac{15}{16}$ inches in diameter,
giving areas approximately equal to 1 square inch, 2 square
inches, and 3 square inches. The test bars were poured at
the same time and under the same conditions. The bars
were broken on bearings 12 inches apart, with the load
applied at the middle. One fact brought out by these tests
is that a bar having 1 square inch section is hardly large
enough to give fair tests of the iron, but it may serve for
comparing very soft grades of iron. Small bars are more
affected than large ones by variations in dampness and other

irregularities in the molds. The test bars were supplied from foundries producing and using the grades of iron mentioned in the table. They all showed a perfectly solid structure at the point of fracture.

TABLE VIII.

COMPARATIVE TESTS OF VARIOUS GRADES OF CAST IRON.

Class of Iron.	Approximate Diameter of Bar. Inches.	Exact Diameter of Bar. Inches.	Area of Bar. Square Inches.	Transverse Breaking Load. Pounds.	Deflection. Inch.
Chilled roll	$1\frac{1}{8}$	1.140	1.021	3,250	.105
	$1\frac{5}{8}$	1.655	2.151	9,500	.090
	$1\frac{15}{16}$	1.968	3.042	15,250	.085
Gun carriage	$1\frac{1}{8}$	1.122	.988	2,780	.100
	$1\frac{5}{8}$	1.664	2.174	9,250	.110
	$1\frac{15}{16}$	1.859	2.714	11,820	.100
Car wheel	$1\frac{1}{8}$	1.174	1.082	2,200	.053
	$1\frac{5}{8}$	1.690	2.244	8,100	.070
	$1\frac{15}{16}$	2.008	3.167	13,500	.072
Heavy machinery	$1\frac{1}{8}$	1.187	1.106	2,800	.092
	$1\frac{5}{8}$	1.705	2.282	7,100	.072
	$1\frac{15}{16}$	2.001	3.143	11,900	.079
Stove plate	$1\frac{1}{8}$	1.182	1.097	2,500	.117
	$1\frac{5}{8}$	1.745	2.391	6,050	.078
	$1\frac{15}{16}$	2.047	3.288	9,900	.081
Bessemer	$1\frac{1}{8}$	1.175	1.084	2,150	.100
	$1\frac{5}{8}$	1.698	2.263	5,500	.100
	$1\frac{15}{16}$	1.991	3.112	8,900	.085
	1 in. sq.	.994	.988	1,757	.150

The majority of the committee appointed by the American Foundrymen's Association to make tests of different grades of iron decided, after making a large number of tests with different sizes of bars, that a 1½-inch round bar is the smallest size that should be used in soft irons, and for hard grades they recommend a 2-inch or a 2½-inch round bar. They also recommend that all test bars be cast on end.

92. Testing the Chill of Cast Iron.—The chilling test is sometimes used as a guide in making up mixtures. If the test is always made in the same mold or against the same chill, and with iron at the same temperature and degree of fluidity, it is evident that the depth of chill will be affected mostly by the chemical composition of the iron, and can thus be relied on to give a pretty fair idea as to the silicon, sulphur, and manganese contents of the metal. Some experimental work is usually necessary to determine the best size and form of mold to use, some metals requiring a larger and some a smaller specimen and chill. In all cases the specimen should be of such thickness that the entire body will not be chilled, some of the metal being left gray and soft. Chill tests may be made in the style of mold shown in Fig. 5, with various modifications, or the specimen may be cast against the flat chill shown in Fig. 6 (*a*). In this case a pattern similar to the one shown in Fig. 6 (*b*) is used. This is placed against the flat chill *a*, Fig. 6 (*a*), thus leaving the space *b* in the mold into which the metal can be poured. In chill tests, the chill should be so placed that the iron will not have a chance to flow over it in any large volume.

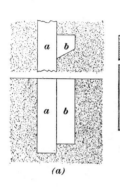

(*b*)

(*a*)

Fig. 6.

The white part denotes the chill, which can be measured, or, if small, judged by the eye. One precaution that must always be followed in chill tests is to see that the same mold or pattern and chill are always used in tests that are to be compared, on account of the fact that the body of metal in the chill will affect the rate of cooling and the physical conditions of the test piece.

93. Fluidity Test of Cast Iron.—In casting test bars it is often important to know the relative fluidity of the metal.

A method for making these determinations is to attach a wedge-shaped strip b, Fig. 7 (a), to the lower end of the pattern for the test bar that is cast vertically. The strip tapers from $\frac{1}{8}$ inch thick at the bar to a knife edge. Fig. 7 (b) shows two test bars cast at once, and so arranged that simultaneous tests may be made of the fluidity, contraction, and chill. The

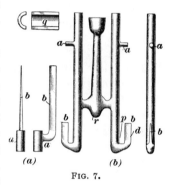

(a)   (b)

FIG. 7.

pieces b for testing the fluidity show that the iron was not sufficiently fluid to entirely fill the mold made by the tapered strips. Circular chills similar to that shown at q may be placed in the molds at the lower end of the test bars. In pouring castings in which there are to be local chills, the gates should be arranged so that no great amount of metal flows over the chills. The tips a and p are accurately cast 12 inches apart in the mold, and with chilled faces, so as to have a clean surface to measure from. By measuring the distance between a and p in the casting, the contraction is determined. Both bars were cast from one gate r and the gates cut in such a manner as to give the iron a spiral or whirling motion as it entered the molds, thus tending to float any dirt to the top. In molding test bars, the tempering of the sand and ramming of the mold should be very carefully attended to, as any variations are liable to cause uneven bars or irregularities in the combined carbon in the different parts of the bar. Care should also be taken in the use of the swab in molds for test bars, as the additional moisture introduced by the swab may affect the bar.

94. Tensile Tests of Cast Iron.—Table VII gives the tensile tests of three grades of cast iron for comparison. These bars were molded on end in green sand and broken

without any special cleaning or preparation except to brush
them free from sand.   It requires more skill than is generally supposed to cast perfect test bars on end.   However,
by arranging a suitable flask, to overcome the difficulties
in getting the iron into the mold, so as to obtain uniform
conditions and bars, very successful results were obtained.
The length of bars for tensile tests is 8 inches between the
grips of the machine.   Thousands of tests have been made
on bars of various dimensions.   The bars were cast in green
sand, dry sand, and in chills.   Also, they were tested both
in the rough and machined to some accurate area, and some
rough bars were given treatment in the tumbling barrels.
The strength of machined bars is less per square inch than
rough bars of the same area; the variation in the strength
of machined bars is as great as that of the rough ones;
tumbling increases the strength of all rough bars.

95.   Measuring Test Bars.—It is not safe to depend
on the size of the pattern in determining the size of the bar,
as differences in rapping the pattern, or in the condition of
the molds, may cause a considerable variation in the size of
the castings obtained from a given pattern.   Hence, all test
bars, whether round or square, should be carefully measured
in order to determine their exact section.   In case of bars
that have been machined, this measuring is usually done
before they are introduced into the testing machine, but
as cast iron does not greatly reduce in cross-section at
the point of fracture, it is good practice to measure the
area of the bar after fracture.   A micrometer is the best
instrument for measuring the areas of test bars.   As a cast-
iron bar may not be a perfect circle, it is necessary to
measure more than one diameter and get the average to use
in calculating the area.   Likewise, bars may not be perfectly square or rectangular, and measurements should be
made across each edge.

The results obtained from any set of tests should be
recorded in tabular form, as shown in Table VII.   The
areas of the bars should be determined, and, in tensile tests,

the breaking load per square inch computed. It is impossible to lay down any general rules for the strength of cast iron that will apply to any section, as its physical characteristics are radically different from those of wrought iron and steel. It is necessary to consider pieces of the same sections and lengths when comparing the strengths.

96. Testing Machines.—For breaking test bars or making deflection tests, a great variety of machines is used. Some shops are provided with elaborate testing machines, with capacities up to 100,000 pounds, driven by hand or by power; but for ordinary comparison work for transverse tests on bars not over $1\frac{1}{4}$ inches square or $1\frac{1}{4}$ inches in diameter, a machine of the style shown in Fig. 8 may be used. In this machine the bar a is placed on supports b and c, and is broken by forcing down the block d

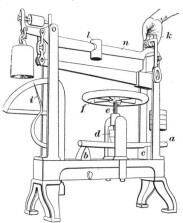

FIG. 8.

by means of the screw e. The pressure is weighed on the scale beam n, and the deflection recorded in thousandths of an inch by means of the pointer i. Unless an automatic poise is used, it is well to keep one hand in the position shown at k, so that any rise of the beam will be noticed and the sliding weight l adjusted immediately. If this precaution is not taken, the beam n may rise quickly and errors of as much as from 200 to 400 pounds be made in reading the breaking load.

97. Autographic Testing Machine. — There are many foundries, for example those making agricultural castings, stove plate, etc., that require daily tests of the casts, or in some cases, one test per week. To get the average iron, the test bars should be poured from that taken about the middle of the heat.   While various sizes of test bars are used by founders, for cheapness of bars and ease and rapidity in operating the testing machine, $\frac{1}{2}$-inch square bars 12 inches long, molded with the gate underneath and with a chill at each end, are a favorite size for some founders.   By making tests of strength, deflection, shrinkage, and chill each day, a record of the best mixture will be obtained, prompt notice is given of any tendency of the mixture to change, and an indication of what is needed to regain the proper standard is obtained; and frequently the cost of the mixture may be lessened and at the same time its quality be improved.   An **autographic testing machine** for breaking small test bars is shown in Fig. 9.   The test bar a,

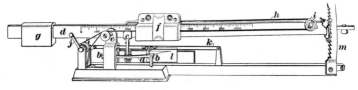

FIG. 9.

$\frac{1}{2}$ inch square and 12 inches long, is fastened at the ends in flexible bearings b, b.   The load is put on the middle of the bar by means of the arm c and the beam d, which is pivoted at e and carries a movable weight f and a counterpoise g. The weight f is propelled forwards or backwards by a steel cord h passing around a pulley i at the end of the beam and attached to the drum and crank j at the rear of the machine. The crank j also operates a cord k that moves a frame with a card l horizontally and in contact with a pencil point attached to the middle of the test bar.   By turning the crank j, the weight f moves along the beam d and gradually applies the load to the test bar a.   The rack m at the end of the machine catches the beam when the bar breaks and prevents any injury to the machine from the shock.   As the weight f moves along the beam d and the test bar bends downwards in the middle, the card l moves horizontally and records the line $a\,b$, shown in Fig. 10, which is a full-size autographic

record of a test bar that broke at 390 pounds. The horizontal line *a c* is made by moving the card *l* in contact with
the pencil before any load is applied to the bar. The per-
pendicular distance *c d* measured between the lines *a b*
and *a c* at any point, as *d*, is the total deflection of the bar
in inches for the load *a c*. The line *a f* is the stress in the
bar, which in this case is 390 pounds, and *b f* is the strain or

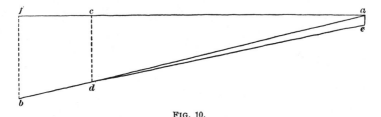

FIG. 10.

distortion in inches in the bar where it broke. When the
stress reached 300 pounds and the strain *c d* was recorded,
the weight *f* was brought back to the starting point and the
card *l* recorded the line *d e*. The distance *a e* is the amount
in inches of permanent set in the bar. The stress was then
applied and the line *e d b* recorded, the bar breaking at
390 pounds, which is represented by the line *a f* in the
diagram.